Monkey on the Bellrope

by Gertrude Caudill

(Gertrude Caudill Dealy Sorlien)

Illustrated by Rudy Bischof

Drift Creek Press
Philomath, Oregon

Monkey on the Bellro
pages will not show tl

M000013847

Copyright © 1992 by Gertrude Caudill

Library of Congress Cataloging-in-Publication Data

Caudill, Gertrude. Monkey on the Bellrope
by Gertrude Caudill.
p. 256 cm. 22 Illustrated.
ISBN 0-9626441-1-0
1. Caudill, Gertrude 2. Women clergy-Northwest, Pacific-
Biography
3. Animal-Monkey-Behavioral
BV676.C3A3 1992

Except for the names of members of the Dealy and Sorlien families and Mrs. Swenson, all other names in this book are fictitious.

Of the trademarked products mentioned in this work, Ford ® is a trademark of Ford Motor Corporation; Kleenex ® and Kleenex Tissues ® are trademarks of Kimberely-Clark Corporation; Sugar Pops ® is a trademark of Kellogg Company.

Published by Drift Creek Press
PO Box 511, Philomath, OR, 97370

Printed and bound in the United States of America

10 9 8 7 6 5 4 3 2 1

Author's Foreward

The first thing I wrote, after I retired and settled into my new home, was an article about Elmer. Elmer was the small Capuchin monkey who had once laughed, turned somersaults, and sprinkled notes of joy into my life.

I read it to Professor Simon Johnson of Oregon State University and the Chintimini Writers' Group, of which I had just become a member.

I feared they might consider my subject frivolous. They didn't.

"We want to hear more about Elmer," they insisted. "Why don't you write a book about him?" So I kept on writing and reading to them each week until the story was completed.

While I wrote to please my friends, there was a deeper reason. I had long felt an incessant urge to write about the amazingly fascinating and intelligent little creature who had contributed so much to the enrichment of my life and the lives of others. I wanted to tell about his interactions with the people around us. And I wanted to perpetuate his vital personality for as many as my words could reach.

When Elmer died, a lot of laughter and tenderness went out of the world of those of us who knew him. Yet Elmer still lives in our memories.

May this book also keep him alive for each of you.

Gertrude Caudill Dealy Sorlien

PS. I have written with love and appreciation for all the wonderful people who were friends of Elmer and me.

Dedicated to

My sons: Paul Dealy, Ross Dealy, Glen Dealy.
My step-daughter, Meredith S. King.
Each of my grandchildren and great-grandchildren.

Contents

Monkey on the Bellrope

≫ 1 ≪

The Gift

"Who on earth is ELMER?" I hung up the phone and stared in bewilderment at the names on the telegraphed message I had just copied. The telegram was from New York:

ARRIVING LOVE FIELD DALLAS 6 PM TODAY.
ROSS GLEN ELMER.

Ross and Glen, the younger of my three sons, were back in the States at last. They would be with me in a few short hours. And the surges of joy that rolled over me were in no way dampened by my confusion over this "Elmer," whoever he was.

Eight months before, the boys, aged nineteen and eighteen, had roared away into the night on their big Indian motorcycles.

"No need to worry about us, Mom!" Glen said. "You just get on with summer classes and we'll be home in time to enroll with you for fall term!"

When I objected that it was not so simple as that, Ross replied, "There's nothing to it! We'll just run down through Mexico and Central America, cross the Panama Canal, then do a tour around South America. We'll be home before you know it!"

But I did worry. Perhaps I was overly concerned for my children due to the grief that still twisted at my heart. My husband, the boys' father, had died suddenly two years before. My oldest son, Paul, was in the service and stationed in the States, so I felt reasonably assured of his safety. But these other two, rushing off heedless and light-hearted into the unknown, were something else. Yet I didn't want to deny them the adventures of life.

Through the summer I attended classes at Southern Methodist University. During breaks in my studies, I visualized Glen and Ross making their way through the dangers of strange cities and bumping over one-way trails in even stranger jungles. And I waited for letters that never came. Well, some of them came, but others did not reach me until long after the boys were home.

My fears, it turned out, were well founded. Ross and Glen had encountered all sorts of adversity. They spent a month on the East Bank of the Panama Canal, waiting for their motorcycles, which a Nicaraguan clerk had carelessly shipped back to Mexico. They were robbed of their money and passports in Lima. They grew ill struggling to fix tires at 12,000 feet in the Andes. And they were benumbed by cold and snow while they labored across the mountains of Southern Argentina.

What's more, they did not get home in time to start the fall term at the University. While I was signing up for classes, they were still working their way down the western section of South America.

But that was past and now they would be with me in a matter of hours! It was Sunday, January 17, 1954, and I felt certain that no church bells in the whole state of Texas rang more joyously than those that chimed in my heart. Yet, I couldn't imagine why the boys were bringing home some stranger named Elmer.

My sister, Dessie, came from her home across town to meet me at the airport. She had shared many a troubled hour with me during those months of suspense, and it was fitting that she should participate in this happy ending.

A Texas Norther whipped at our skirts and snow was beginning to sift down as we stood outside at Dallas's Love Field and watched the plane circle for its landing. In spite of the cold, Dessie's habitual good cheer dimpled and danced across her upturned face. I stood rubbing my hands together as much from excitement as from the need to keep warm.

"How are you going to put this 'Elmer' up for the night?" she asked.

"I don't know. The friends I'm staying with have told me the boys can occupy their spare room for a few days, but they certainly don't have accommodations for anyone else. I can't imagine these kids bringing someone home with them. They must think we still live in our big old farmhouse."

The plane began another loop around the field. We watched it circle, oblivious to the crowd that jostled about us.

"I sure hope Elmer speaks English," I mumbled.

"He probably doesn't," Dessie said.

"Doesn't what?" I replied absently.

"Elmer probably doesn't speak English. He's probably one of those Indians right out of the interior of Brazil with nothing to his name but a G-string and a blowgun."

"Be pretty chilly for him in this weather," I said. We chuckled at the idea. Then the plane began its final approach and I threw my arms joyously about my sister. "They're landing! I don't care who they have with them, I just want to get my eyes on those sons of mine!"

The boys were easy to spot in the smartly dressed crowd that flowed down the steps from the plane. They were a couple of skinny, battered-looking youngsters moving along under enormous, jauntily colored South American hats. Glen carried a new guitar while Ross was singularly attentive to a small pink box.

In the midst of our welcoming hugs, Dessie suddenly stood back and looked around. "Hey, you guys, where's your friend Elmer?" she asked.

The boys grinned at each other. "Let's get in out of this cold," Glen said, "and we'll introduce you to him."

Once inside, Dessie and I surveyed the lounge. The men we saw were mostly the tall Texan type. Surely none of these came from South America.

Ross had seated himself and with Glen hovering at his shoulder, was methodically removing the string from the pink box. This was similar in size to a bakery cake box, but I noticed it had holes punched in it.

Suddenly the box was open, and I gasped as Ross drew forth a tiny, live thing with great, terror-glazed eyes.

"Meet Elmer, Mom!" my sons chimed as they held out to me this diminutive creature of black hair and eyes.

"He's our coming-home present for you!" they said, but their words were almost drowned out by the clamor of baby squalling with which Elmer split the air.

Dessie and I stared at the boys and their gift in utter astonishment. Finally I stammered, "Wh—What is it?"

"Why, he's a baby monkey," Ross replied, turning his charge away from the lights and stroking him gently.

Glen got in a few pats, then said, "We sold our motorcycles when we got to Rio, and after we bought our tickets home, we had ten dollars left. So we went out and blew it on this present for you!"

My sons looked very pleased with themselves, but I was appalled. If there was anything in the world I did not need or want right then, it was a baby monkey. I could not keep him—that was a foregone conclusion. But I did not say so at that moment, being too deliriously happy over the return of these two globe-trotters.

We parted from Dessie and returned to my room. The boys placed the pink box before the glowing gas heater, then went to shed their beat-up travel clothes and bathe. In the meantime, I scurried about to beg a larger box and a square of warm blanket from my hostess. These I handed to Ross and Glen when they emerged, scrubbed and glowing, in clean clothes. "Better fix your little monk a bed in this box. He'll be much more comfortable."

The tiny jungle baby objected shrilly as he was moved to the larger box. But once in his new quarters he settled down, soothed by the soft blanket and a return to the dark.

For hours I plied my sons with questions about their arduous trip, finally assuring myself that despite their gaunt appearance, they seemed to be in reasonably good shape. Only then did I get around to the gift.

"You know, fellas," I said as gently as I could, " we'll just have to donate that baby monkey to the zoo."

They snapped out of their torpor. "What? Don't you like our present?"

"Oh, I do very much appreciate the gift," I hastened to say. "The point is, there's simply no room in my life at this time for a monkey. If we were still on the farm, I'd gladly keep him. But my friends invited me to room here only while you two were gone, so just as soon as tests are over, I have to start looking for another place to stay. And who is going to take in a woman with a monkey? Most folks just won't rent to people with pets."

The boys started to object, but I hurried on. "And there's the fact of my being in school. I don't have the time to raise him. What's more, I don't have the slightest idea how to care for a monkey, or what to feed him, or anything!"

"Oh, Mom, you worry too much," replied Ross. "I'm sure you'll work out something about a place to live, and you'll figure out some sort of schedule that will include Elmer along with literature and theology and all the rest."

Glen added, "Feeding the monkey won't be a problem; the man we bought him from told us to just put a banana in with him and he'd be okay."

Then he flashed me a devilish grin and said, "You like bananas anyway, don't you, Mom!" I smiled at his roguery.

We sat in silence for a few moments, savoring the coziness of the warm room while the Norther moaned outside and the wind-tossed branches scraped at the windows. How good it was to at last have my two sons here in this room, safe and unharmed. In comparison, the problem of the monkey was a minor thing, but it *was* a problem.

There was still another reason for not keeping the monkey, which I had not mentioned. In a year and a half, I would be out of school and back in Washington State, where I expected to be ordained and then appointed to serve as minister of a church. A woman minister in 1954 was curiosity enough without the encumbrance of a monkey!

True, I had served a parish a few years ago and received warm acceptance. But in view of prevailing public attitudes, those people, I felt, were unusual. My next pastorate might well be different. A monkey was the last thing I needed in the effort to establish myself in a new community.

At midnight, my sons stood up and yawned. Then, with tender grins, they peered in at their sleeping baby.

"He is a cute one," I said. "Too bad we can't keep him."

Ross and Glen looked knowingly at each other and went lightheartedly off to bed. I read that look. It said, "We know our mother. She'll find a way, she'll keep him."

My children seemed to have developed the idea that their mother could do anything she set her mind to, a holdover, I reflected, from the simpler days of their childhood. Well, if those two were old enough to go to college and to travel around continents, then they were certainly old enough to understand that some things were impossible. That little monk would have to go.

≫ 2 ≪

Temporary Baby

I turned the gas heater a little lower. It would have to be left on all night. Even Dallas's normally mild winters would be too cold for this baby from the tropics, and we were having abnormally cold temperatures. As I moved his box a little closer to the stove, the tiny monkey whimpered forlornly. The sound tugged at my heart. Nevertheless, I resolved that I would put up with my small guest just this one night—no more.

Joy and excitement over the return of Ross and Glen had completely erased from my mind the thought of those final exams that were to begin the next day. The inevitable had to be faced. But it was after midnight and I was in no mood to study, so I set the alarm clock to ring at four a.m. and collapsed into bed.

The sound that awakened me, however, did not come from the clock, but from the box by the heater. It was like the thin, dreary wailing of a forsaken human baby. I couldn't stand it.

I sprang out of bed and in double-quick time, turned up the heat and put a pan of milk on the stove to warm. Then I took the monkey from his box and began to cuddle and reassure him. As I held him gently, the wailing gradually subsided to jerky little sobs and then whimpers. Holding him there close to the heat, I marveled at his lightness. There seemed to be no weight to him at all. He was only a live softness in my hand. Like a new-born human baby, he looked old, only more so. He looked like a diminutive caricature of a wizened old man.

The boys had told me that the person who sold Elmer to them claimed the monkey was over three months old and ate on his own. Yet when I looked at that banana in his box, and saw those pitifully ineffective little tooth marks on it, I realized with a pang that this poor baby had no idea how to eat and had been taken directly from its mother. No wonder he cried and sobbed, for not only was he lost and lonely, he was starving. He'd had nothing to eat for at least two days and a night. This, even more than his infancy, would account for his ancient, shriveled appearance.

When I placed the pan of milk on the floor before him, the monkey stopped his whimpering and, after a moment of hesitation, awkwardly sank his small mouth into it. After a few greedy gulps, he came up gasping for air and trying to get the milk out of his nose. Again he plopped his face into the pan and came up wheezing. At this point he sat straight up, popped a tiny thumb in his mouth, and gave that milk his long and puzzled consideration. Clearly he was not accustomed to getting his meals in this manner.

Elmer (it was about at this point that he became Elmer to me) looked up and addressed a few babytalk remarks at me about this new situation. Then he dived in for a few more gulps and came up for another thumbsucking session. He kept up this procedure until he was balloon-bellied and content.

Breakfast over, he went hopping around me while I sat there on the floor and watched him. I was fascinated by his babyness, his ears, and his hands. He was strikingly like a small piece of humanity with a scanty covering of hair. Even his intermittent chatter had something convincingly human in it. He made small consoling sounds, and seemed to be reassuring himself and me that now everything was going to be all right.

After a time he came and cuddled against me while he sucked the tiny thumb of one hand and closed his other hand tight around one of my fingers. I stroked him tenderly and mentally summoned forth all my common-sense arguments against him.

Back from school late that morning, I found that the boys had just gotten out of bed and were fishing Elmer from his box. But the monkey baby saw only danger from these quarters, and he turned into a screaming, kicking, biting fury.

Then he saw me! In a flash he streaked across the room and up to my shoulder. He put his two small arms tight around my neck, stopped his crying, and gave a tiny, gulping sigh. Then, from this refuge, Elmer chattered a smug, scolding challenge at the boys that said plainly, "See, I've got someone to protect me; just you try anything on me now!" He then tucked his thumb in his mouth, snuggled his head close against my neck, and settled down for some peace and comfort.

While Elmer clung to me, I stood looking down at my sons, who were still on the floor by the monkey box.

"Why do you suppose this little monkey is so terrified of you fellows?"

"Well, look, Mom," Ross replied. "We're the ones who took him away from his happy home. We boxed him up and put him on that rattley old Constellation, and it was a long, scary ride from Brazil to La Guardia Field. Cold, too!" He hunched his shoulders with a shuddery b-r-r-r. "So I guess Elmer holds all that stuff against us."

After a moment, he added, "But he's also got it in for us for something else."

Here, Glen took up the account. "Yes, it was what occurred in the men's room at La Guardia Field that really shook him up."

"Oh? What happened?" I asked, as I took a chair near them.

"Well, we went in there to take Elmer out of his box and give him a drink. We figured he must be awfully thirsty after all those hours without water."

"Not only was he thirsty," I interrupted, "do you realize that this poor little thing had nothing to eat from the time you took him from his home in Belem until four o'clock this morning? Just look at that banana in his box. You can see he tried, but he didn't know how to eat it."

Ross and Glen peered at the nibbled but intact banana. The expressions on their faces went from curiosity to profound shock.

Ross said, "Gol-lee, why didn't we notice that last night? The man who sold him to us said all he needed was a banana. Why, that little fellow went without anything at all to eat for over thirty hours!"

"And he also went without anything to drink," Glen said.

"You mean he didn't drink when you offered him water?"

"Heck no! He didn't seem to like it when we sort of held him upside down to drink out of the washbowl. I guess he was just scared. Anyway, he wiggled and carried on like mad, and all at once he got out of our hands and went streaking up the wall. From then on it was pure bedlam. The walls were real high, and Elmer went screeching round and round a narrow ledge up near the ceiling. We were scared he'd go through the door each time it opened. But he was afraid to come down even to the top of the door. Every guy who didn't have to hurry off to catch the next plane stayed to see the show and tried to help. We all stood on radiators, washbowls, and johns, and even climbed the stall walls, but we just couldn't reach that racing little demon."

"So how did you ever catch him?" I asked.

"Well, we finally found a long broom, and we batted him down."

I gasped!

"We *had* to do it, Mom," he said, reacting to my exclamation. "There was just no other way. 'Bout took the wind out of him, too."

"Poor little guy," the boys echoed as they reached to give the monkey conciliatory strokes. They drew back, however, when Elmer screeched deafening defiance and tightened his grip around my neck.

We all laughed, but it was sympathetic laughter. This tiny baby had had just too much to cope with in his young life. Right then, by all rights, he should have been somewhere in a safe nook in the forest nestled close against his mother. But here he was in this alien environment, after all those harrowing experiences, and on top of everything he had nearly starved to death.

While I put milk on the heater to warm, I explained to my sons that it was no wonder the monkey hadn't drunk that water they tried to give him, for in addition to being hung upside down over it, he didn't even know how to drink.

"Tell you what," I added, "I have to take another final exam at two o'clock. While I'm gone, I want you fellows to take the car downtown and shop in the dime stores until you find a doll bottle that's just the right size for Elmer."

They objected that they would look pretty silly shopping for a *doll* bottle. However, I knew that underneath it all their sympathy for the monkey made them want to atone in some way for the misery they had put him through. Sure enough, when I came home late that afternoon, they triumphantly presented me with two miniature one-ounce doll bottles.

"They're just the right size for our baby," I said, then added as I went for the milk, "our temporary baby!"

⇒ 3 ⇐

No Monkeys!

I didn't rush Elmer to the zoo after all. In view of his terrifying experiences, I felt that the little fellow had endured all he could for the time being. And since he felt so secure with me, it seemed only right that he should have a brief respite before another change.

On the day final exams ended, I told Elmer, "The time has come. We must do something to find you another home." But he ran trustingly to my shoulder, nestled under my chin, hugged my neck and baby-talked at me. Then he stuck his thumb in his mouth.

I melted.

Well, I wouldn't do anything drastic at present. I would simply let events bring their own answers.

I had to find another place to live right away, and there was little likelihood that I'd find a place where monkeys were allowed. But I would try. The results would surely prove to me and the boys that Elmer had to be given up.

Poor, trusting little fellow! I held him in my lap and gently tickled his round stomach. He lay on his back, kicking the air, and looked as blissful and contented as any human baby with a full stomach and someone to love him.

I observed that all those bottles of milk had paid off. Elmer now looked like a baby instead of a dried up old man, even though he was still small enough to curl up inside a teacup.

The next morning I set out, armed with addresses of rooms for rent. The first place I approached was a large, elegant brick house on a beautiful tree-lined street, just off from the University. This would be a fine place to live, I thought.

However, once inside I wasn't so certain. The scent of stale cabbage, mingled with other undefinable cooking odors, nearly overpowered me as I climbed the once grand staircase. I followed the faded landlady down a dark hall to a dingy room with peeling wallpaper and tired curtains. It was furnished with a bed, a chest of drawers, a table, and a hot plate, all of which had seen better days. I noted that the room was large enough for my needs, that the windows, once washed, would be sufficient to let in plenty of light. The oak floor also needed thorough cleaning, then it would be okay with a rug or two.

"We never rented out rooms when my husband, Dr. Rockford, was alive," the landlady lamented, fingering a straggle of greying hair. "All the children were home then, coming and going with their friends. Oh, this was a lively place, I can tell you!"

Perhaps she caught me appraising the unwashed curtains, for she added, "In those days we had plenty of maids to do the work."

Then she came back to the business at hand. "This is really a very nice room, but the couple that just moved out didn't appreciate it a single bit. In fact, they complained all the time. Nothing ever suited them. And they didn't get along with each other, either. Why, you should have heard the awful things they said, and how they fought! I know. Many's the time I stood out there in the hall and heard everything that went on!" She clicked her tongue and shook her head. "It was scandalous!"

She looked me over critically as she asked, "You say you don't have either a husband or a roommate?"

I told her I was a widow, and that I did not plan to have a roommate. Then I corrected myself.

"Well, I do have a tiny baby monkey, if you can call him a roommate."

As I said this, I was thinking to myself that I was not enamored with either the room or the landlady, but I might as well get her reaction to Elmer.

I got it.

The woman rolled her pale eyes toward the smokey ceiling and threw up her hands in horror. "A monkey? Never! I have enough trouble with people who won't clean up after themselves, who beat me out of rent, and fight with each other. No dirty, screaming, thieving monkey for me!" And she stamped self-righteously down the stairs ahead of me.

As I left, I couldn't help but wonder if a baby monkey wouldn't be just the thing to revitalize that woman's life. It would give her something positive to think about and care for, something to love her and make her laugh.

I went to another address, and another, and another. Most of them proved to be variations of the first: fine old mansions, some of red brick, some of wood painted white, and all with rooms to let by once affluent people. Sometimes there was an aged, retired professor and his wife, but it was more likely to be the widow. All too often, it seemed that these people had become picky, gossipy, and soured against humanity. I felt considerable compassion for them, however, as I pondered on how their lives had been narrowed by circumstances to the point where they could no longer see beyond the faded walls of their mansions and the faults and foibles of the renters.

These individuals were also alike in their reactions to a monkey. They wouldn't have one! Even the managers of the few professionally built and run rooming houses I visited agreed on this.

Ross and Glen, who had by now moved into dorms, dropped by to see us that evening. Elmer sat on my lap and peacefully picked at the flowered print of my skirt while I reported the experiences of the day and then concluded, "I just don't see any way of keeping this little monkey."

The boys were unconvinced. As they left they said, "You're certain to work something out, Mom!"

They simply refused to accept the idea that Elmer would have to go. To tell the truth, with every passing day, that monkey took more territory in my heart.

Like now. There he lay, again on his back with his thumb in his mouth while he fastened round, trusting eyes on my face.

He still reminded me disturbingly of a scaled-down human baby.

It was almost time for the second semester of school to begin and I went room hunting daily. The results were all the same; they wouldn't let me have a monkey as a roommate. By now, giving up Elmer had become almost unthinkable, yet getting a place to live where he would be accepted seemed impossible.

I finally became reckless and decided to take him with me on one more round of room hunting. The results could be no worse than they had been previously.

Even though the weather had returned to its usual mildness, Elmer shivered when taken outside. So that morning, I wrapped him snugly before I set out on foot for still another address. To my surprise I found myself going up the walk to an entirely different type of house. It was a low, white bungalow, and Mrs. Swenson, the white-haired lady who met me at the door, looked kind and motherly.

"Come right in!" she said cheerily, as she ushered me into her bright kitchen. Two golden cocker spaniels raced in from an adjoining room, stood up and planted their forepaws against me.

"Get down, you two!" she scolded affectionately, as both dogs sniffed with tail-wagging frenzy.

"Down, Tom! Down, Pat!" she again commanded, and then apologized. "I don't know what has come over these two. They're usually well-behaved and—"

Mrs. Swenson broke off suddenly as the tiny bundle I carried began to move. A miniature head popped out, followed by arms, and then the rest of Elmer wriggled free. The dogs went wild!

The woman's face was a model of astonishment as she lifted her voice above the clamor of the dogs to ask, "What is it?"

"It's a baby monkey!" I yelled.

I couldn't see her expression as she bent, seized the cockers and dragged them to an adjoining room. I waited in suspense. Firmly closing the door, she turned again to me and the monkey.

She was smiling gently.

"Could I hold him?" she asked.

Elmer snuggled and crooned himself right into Mrs. Swenson's generous heart. She cuddled him softly against her cheek for a few moments, then looked up at me with shining eyes.

"You know, I came from a farm in Kansas where we always had baby calves or puppies or kittens, something young to care for. I loved them all. But this little thing—umm, he's something!"

Still holding him, she bustled over to put the coffee pot on. Then she pulled out a chair and urged, "Sit down, do sit down! Let's have a cup of coffee!"

We were soon drinking coffee and chuckling over Elmer's antics. He sat straight up on the table and smacked down milk from the doll bottle I'd brought along. After a time, Mrs. Swenson put down her cup and said persuasively, "I do hope you'll rent my room, dear. You and I could be good friends. And I would so love to have Elmer around."

Would I! I hadn't even seen the room yet, but Elmer and I were both in love with Mrs. Swenson, and I was prepared to take any cubbyhole she offered. Before showing me the room she explained that her son, his wife and their two cockers occupied the west section of her house, and it was the front room of her section that was for rent. Her former roomer had just completed his schooling and moved out.

I was delighted with the room. It was big, airy, and clean, with large windows on both the north and east, and it opened onto a porch that stretched invitingly across the front.

Well, there were still problems to solve, like how I'd go to school and at the same time mother a baby monkey as well as other issues that belonged to the future. But at least we now had a place to live!

⇒ 4 ⇐

Who's the Captive?

Once settled in at Mrs. Swenson's, I took stock of my situation. Might as well admit it, I was stuck! Against all reason and common sense, I had become hopelessly entrapped by the round, trusting eyes and wispy, clinging fingers of a baby monkey. Ross remarked sagely to Glen that "this is going to be a most interesting scientific experiment, to see whether Mom brings Elmer up to her standards, or vice versa."

Already this tiny creature, almost a nonentity in size, was making momentous changes in my life. School would never again be the same. Only time would tell what complications he might inject once I became active in my career as a minister.

It had become amply evident that Elmer could not be "hidden under a bushel." He needed fresh air, food, companionship, and entertainment. Everything a developing human baby required. When one of those needs was not forthcoming, he was quick to call it to my attention, or if need be, to the attention of the whole world. One day I stayed after class to confer with a professor. On my return home, a neighbor whom I had known only by sight met me a block from the house. Standing there with eyes snapping and arms akimbo, she reprimanded me severely. "*Where have you been?* You're a whole hour late and Elmer's been crying his head off!"

The monkey, lonesome and hungry—though not too hungry, since I always left extra food in his cage—had informed all the neighbors of his plight. My heart warmed toward the woman next door for caring enough about my monkey to scold me.

During my pre-Elmer school life, I had reveled in long hours of study at the library. Now, however, I had to quickly check out the books I needed and rush home. Even when summer brought record high temperatures, I could not retreat to that lovely, air chilled sanctum. Instead, I came home and, night and day, dripped perspiration over stacks of books and papers. Elmer, meanwhile, played, took his meals, or slept, and did not mind the heat.

Mrs. Swenson once mentioned that if I left my door unlocked, she would be glad to look after Elmer whenever she was home. I declined her kindhearted offer however, since she did babysitting and was often gone herself. More to the point, she had several grandchildren who came and went and found touching the monkey an irresistible temptation. Elmer would have been terrified had they rushed in, poking and squealing, during my absence. And, fragile and nearly weightless though he was, he did have one effective means of defense—tiny, needle-sharp eye teeth. I didn't want Mrs. Swenson's grandchildren going around with punctured fingers.

The monkey also whittled down my social life, especially when it came to evenings out. At that stage in life he was afraid of being alone at night, even with the lights on.

The first evening that I left him alone stands out in my memory. I was going to a concert with a friend.

"You have to learn to stay alone some time," I told him.

Elmer clutched my fingers, twined himself around my wrist, and objected strenuously to being put back into his cage. He had come to regard evening as our togetherness time and this was an outrage.

When I picked up my handbag, fright was added to outrage. He put up a racket of squalling that sounded exactly like a distressed human baby. All my coaxing and soothing was to no avail. I finally closed the door to the sound of those infant screams and the sight of a small, pleading face and tiny upreaching arms.

I went away feeling like the lowest creature in existence, and my self-esteem was not improved by the scene upon my return. There was only a deep silence when I put the key in the door, none of the happy chatter that usually greeted me. Elmer huddled in a far corner of his cage and his eyes were fear-glazed, so much so that for a few moments he didn't even seem to know me. Then, as I stroked and talked to him, the corners of his mouth began to quiver. But he uttered no sound. The poor little fellow had evidently cried until he couldn't cry anymore. I held him against my cheek while he gradually relaxed and at last began to make small self-assuring murmurs.

If Elmer subtracted things from my life, he also added compensations. My former life, often grief-filled and lonely, now took on zip and brightness, for Elmer, in his exuberant babyhood, allowed no sadness or loneliness to prevail for long.

Breakfast, which had once been just something to get through quickly, now became an occasion, since Elmer insisted on sharing it. By seven o'clock each morning, the little monk was all washed, diapered and sitting on the table. While I sipped coffee, Elmer took his doll bottle of milk. Holding the bottle in both hands, he leaned far back on his heels and teetered precariously while he downed his milk. This done, he promptly yanked the nipple off the bottle and carefully investigated to make certain the milk was all gone. Having assured himself on this score, he gave the bottle a careless fling and then climbed to his own private perch, a green up-side-down bowl. From this point on we conversed companionably across the table, looking at each other over our slices of toast with blackberry jam—mine regular sized, Elmer's cut to scale.

I never knew what to expect from Elmer. I was tuned in to the small sounds he made in play, and once, when things had become just too quiet, I sprang up to search. When I found him, the monkey was dangling head down in the coffee pot. He had himself neatly tail-anchored to the top of the handle while he trailed his fingers in the cold coffee.

My apartment now wore an habitual tipsy look. Lamp shades sat at jaunty angles, pictures hung awry, and strange things happened. A curtain might shudder oddly, or a piece of clothing might stretch itself full-length and slither across the floor. One day I was brought out of my books by a

tearing, clattering sound. Elmer was streaking gleefully across the floor with an agitated spiral of typewriter ribbon unwinding behind him.

A common sight was a section of newspaper gone wild. It raced madly up and down the room, under the bed, over stacks of books and anything else in its path. Underneath all the crackle and flutter, one might now and then glimpse a shining eye, or the tip of a black tail.

One day while picking up after one of those newspaper sprees, I thought about all that was involved in having the monkey. Aside from such things as hurrying home from school to keep him company, fishing him out of the coffeepot, rewinding the typewriter ribbon, and numberless other pick-up periods like this, there were all those hours spent in giving Elmer baths, taking him for walks, feeding him four times a day, and chasing him down to rescue a new blouse, a watch, or a freshly typed theme. Was he really worth it?

When the room was back in order, I turned to look at the object of my woes. There he lay in bed, all tired innocence. He was leisurely kicking his feet in the air while he sucked the thumb of one hand and scratched his belly with the other. All the while he followed my every move with adoring baby eyes.

I dissolved! He reminded me sharply of my babies from a few brief years ago. I certainly wouldn't have admitted this out loud, however. I still carried a mental picture from my rural childhood of a befurred rich woman mincing down a city street cuddling a poodle. People spoke with disparagement of "the idle rich," and inferred that such a woman was somehow too lazy and lacking in human love to have her own children and therefore lavished all that attention on a mere dog.

My background had instilled within me the idea that animals were supposed to be...well, just animals. Dogs were to round up cows, cats were to catch mice. And a person was not, for goodness sake, to put them on a par with people. It's true that in my parents' home, and later in my own, there was a great feeling of kinship with animals. In spite of everything, we still grew attached to our dogs, cats, chickens, turkeys, goats and calves. We delighted in recounting such tales as the smart tricks of Old Bess, the cow who learned to unfasten the barn door and who often went in to help herself to an early supper. But when that same Old Bess was no longer profitable as a milk producer, she was summarily sent to the butcher. No room for sentiment, it had to be done.

Therefore I masked my fondness for the monkey, or tried to. But the first day that I ventured down to the shopping center with him, my disguise fell. On the way, I met a person right out of my childhood.

In order to save time, I had decided to give the monkey his outings by combining them with errands. On this day I planned to make a quick jaunt to the Snider Plaza grocery store—just rush in for a loaf of bread and a quart of milk and be out again. As we left the house, Elmer settled down on my shoulder, put his arms tight around my neck, and surveyed the world with smug aloofness as we moved down the street.

I hurried along and was nearly to the grocery store when I saw a woman stalking toward me with disapproval in every line of her body. She stopped directly in front of me and demanded to know how I could *stand* that horrible creature against my neck.

For some reason, I wasn't particularly angry. Rather, I felt a sort of detached interest in her impertinence. "Oh, I don't mind at all having this little monkey against my neck," I replied pleasantly. Then, perversely out of character, I teased, "As a matter of fact, I like it. He's *so* nice and cuddly."

A grimace pulled the corners of the woman's mouth almost to her collar, but she continued to block my way and glare. Finally she spoke again, accusingly. "Of course, you don't have any children."

"Oh, but I do!" I affirmed. "Three grown sons."

While she gasped and sputtered over this information, I slipped around her and continued on my way. There it was, I thought, the old fur-coat-and-poodle mind set. I wondered how much more of this type of thinking Elmer and I would encounter.

Inside the store, before we were half-way to the milk cartons, we were completely surrounded by laughing, questioning shoppers.

"What is it?" they wanted to know.

"A baby monkey," I replied.

"What kind of monkey?" they asked.

By now I had studied up on monkeys and was able to tell them he was a Capuchin, the so-called "Organ Grinder" monkey. Amid all the questions and hilarity, Elmer maintained his wide-eyed, infant sobriety and only once broke his silence. That was for a man to whom he took a special liking. Standing straight up and holding firmly to a lock of my hair, he looked his new friend in the eye and chattered up a storm while his audience cheered.

However, the monkey could also develop an instant aversion to someone. When a squealy woman edged in between him and his new friend and tried to poke him in the stomach and tweak his ears, Elmer clammed up and used his own methods for getting rid of her. First he gave with the glassy stare. When this failed, he turned his back. The woman went prancing around me to look him in the face, only to find herself again staring at his back. Around in front again—the same view. To the back—still the same. For her, the monkey had become only a back and tail.

The crowd had scattered enough for me to inch along. We got our milk and were on the way to the bread rack when a pudgy little lady, all abeam, bore down upon us. She pushed me into a spot between the bread and the grapefruit and then commanded breathlessly, "Now, listen, honey, you stay *right there!* My children are in the car just a block up. I'll bring them. They've *got* to see that monkey!"

I waited, thinking that I ought to get myself an organ and Elmer a tin cup. While waiting I also marveled at the kind of behavior one small monkey could produce in human beings. What else could cause that woman to demand a perfect stranger to stand in one spot until she returned? For that matter, what else could make me stand there?

I chuckled to myself as I remembered my sons' remarks about Elmer being a scientific experiment as to whose standards would prevail. Whose indeed? Certainly he had worked changes in my whole lifestyle and even in my way of thinking. Not only that, he seemed to bring out unusual behavior and attitudes in everyone we met.

Even my bright young sons were not immune to Elmer's influence. I thought of this again the day Ross, Glen and I attended a show at the Dallas Ice Skating Arena. When the star of the show, Sonja Henie, glided by in swan-like grace with her bespangled costume and bare shoulders glimmering under the blue spotlights, we gasped at the beauty of the scene. Then Glen leaned toward me and whispered, "She'd be *perfect* if she just had a monkey around her neck!"

⟫ 5 ⟪

Eggheads

Such was Elmer's effect on me that I now tended to divide the world into two kinds of people: those who liked monkeys and those who did not. Occasionally someone who disliked monkeys would pass by with a stony stare and let it go at that, but most felt impelled to stop me and deliver their opinions on the subject. The vast majority of people I met, however, were monkey-lovers. These could be recognized a half block away, for they approached with progressively softening features. After they had gone by they still wore that gentle, grinning "seen-a-monkey" expression. It somehow gave me confidence in the human race.

I continued to take Elmer down to Snider Plaza, though by now I had learned to allow more time for errands. The place was patronized mainly by students and townspeople. I had never met any of the school's personnel there, and that was fine with me, since I had a vague fear that once I was seen with the monkey, I might be singled out as an eccentric.

Then one sunny day in April, when I was about to enter the drugstore with Elmer on my shoulder, I heard myself being paged from up the street.

My psychology professor, Dr. Yorkman, a rather smallish man wreathed in perpetual good humor, was calling.

"Mrs. Dealy, Mrs. Dealy! Wait!" Then, as he came up to me, he gasped, "What *is* that on your shoulder?"

I gave Elmer a reassuring pat as I replied, "This is a baby monkey, and his name is Elmer."

"You don't say! I was beginning to wonder if they'd spiked that cup of coffee I just drank!"

Then, twinkling and chuckling, the professor reached out to Elmer and coaxed, "Hey there, Elmer Baby, come to Grandpa."

As Elmer timidly tightened his hold around my neck, the professor said, "I'm a brand-new grandfather! What do you think of that?"

Without waiting for my reply, he went on. "It's a girl and her name's Irene. She's cute, too. Resembles her granddad. Oh, and she weighs eight pounds, two ounces."

"She's got Elmer beat there," I said. "He barely tips the scales at nine ounces, and he's seven months old!"

Dr. Yorkman gave the monkey a few tentative strokes as he said, "Well, for such a little guy, he's certainly good-looking."

"Yes, he looks like me, don't you think, Dr. Yorkman?

The professor squinted intently at Elmer. "Darned if he doesn't!" he declared solemnly. "Dark eyes, dark hair, nice smooth face. He's a little darker complexioned than you, though!" We stood there and laughed idiotically as patrons of the drugstore jostled around us.

The next day, going down the hall after my psychology class, Dr. Yorkman caught up with me again.

"How's your baby, Mrs. Dealy?"

"Just fine, Dr. Yorkman. How's your granddaughter?"

From then on, this was our standard formula of greeting, always followed with the latest news of the two babies. When Irene had gained one pound, Elmer had gained only a fraction of an ounce.

But by the time Baby Irene's wandering blue eyes focused for the first time on the bright bauble tied to her crib, Elmer had long since spotted and raced for every tiny object that glittered. He even tried to catch sunbeams.

One Monday morning after class and our usual banter about babies, Dr. Yorkman asked, "What's the matter with your eye, Mrs. Dealy? It looks irritated."

"I had a little mishap," I replied. "But I'm on my way right now to the doctor. I'll tell you about it Wednesday."

The eye episode had started on the previous Friday afternoon while Ross, Glen and I sat visiting on the front porch. With Elmer on my lap, I listened to the boys tell of all the latest happenings over at their dorm.

I was only dimly aware that Elmer was looking intently into my eyes. Suddenly, with the speed of light, he shot out a small hand and grabbed at my eyeball. Although he partially succeeded, it didn't really hurt and the boys and I just sat back and laughed.

Later that evening, however, my eye started to hurt a little. By Sunday it was swollen and so painful that I was unable to study. This was serious since my study schedule didn't allow for time off. I therefore went over to the school clinic, where a nurse bandaged my eye and told me to come back the next day when a doctor would be in.

When I entered the doctor's office after Dr. Yorkman's class, I looked carefully at the physician, hoping that he was the kind of person who would laugh with me over this monkey-and-eye incident. He was doing something with a few instruments at a counter and his back was partially turned to me when he asked in a preoccupied tone, "What's the matter with your eye?"

I felt foolish and laughed nervously as I explained, "Well, Doctor, I have a little monkey over at my place. Last Friday he tried to grab my eyeball and I guess he scratched it."

By the time I finished speaking, the doctor was facing me, unsmiling and utterly silent. After a time he proceeded to carefully examine my eye. Then, still silent, he cleansed, medicated, and bandaged it. Finally, he stood back and looked down at me from beneath drawn-together black eyebrows.

He spoke, spacing out his words. "I don't want you to even look inside of a book for at least three days. It may take longer but come back here at that time and we'll see. And also," here, his voice rose, "get rid of that monkey!"

I got up and stumbled to the door. As I went out, he roared, "GET RID OF THAT MONKEY!"

Walking back across campus, I wondered what had made the doctor react with such hostility at the mention of a monkey. Was he overly tired? Had he had trouble with someone just before he saw me? Or could it possibly be that he once had an unfortunate experience with a monkey? I would never know, because I didn't intend to go back there.

At home, Elmer welcomed me with much happy crooning and snuggling. I returned his caresses and said, "Get rid of you, Elmer? No sirree! You didn't mean to hurt my eye, did you? You just wanted to take it out and play with it."

I tickled his stomach gently. "Can you imagine, little guy? You have an enemy over at the Health Center. Well, that doctor said for me to report back to him, but I'm not going. I think I shall take as my motto, 'Love me, love my monkey.'"

In answer, Elmer darted to my shoulder and set to work nimbly peeling a strip of tape from the eye patch. No matter. As it turned out, I didn't need the patch for long. My eye healed rapidly and in a couple of days I was back on a full schedule of study.

After my psychology class on Wednesday, Dr. Yorkman and I again compared notes on our babies. Then he demanded, "Now tell me about that eye!"

I gave him the account and mentioned the strange behavior of the doctor. The professor gave a long, low whistle and then grinned wryly. "Sounds like a good case study for Abnormal Psychology, doesn't it? Human behavior makes you wonder sometimes who really is progressing up the evolutionary scale." The laugh lines creased around his eyes as he added, "Tell you what. Why don't you do a study for me about the kind of reactions Elmer sets off in your professors and the college personnel in general?"

We both laughed, knowing that he more than half meant it. As I walked down the hall, he called, "Report back to me on that assignment!"

I kept Elmer away from the campus and had almost forgotten Dr. Yorkman's teasing assignment until an incident that occurred some time later.

Elmer's sprightly mood must have begun early to rub off on me. I don't know how else to explain the fact that one summer day I actually had the temerity to march right into the austere precincts of the School of Theology with the monkey riding jauntily on my shoulder.

Perkins School of Theology stood lofty and chaste on the south side of campus, its quietness a solemn contrast to the teeming activity of the rest of the university. Oh, there were people here, gliding about beneath the upreaching chapel spire, but the whole mood was entirely different—serene, subdued.

I went directly to the professor's office where I had an appointment. The cool, dark aura of books, mahogany, and ivied windows enfolded us as I paused just inside the room. Elmer, feeling the strangeness, pushed close against my cheek. Then an inner door opened and in walked the distinguished Dr. Corey.

He did a quick double-take, then brushed back his shock of wavy white hair while his eyes crinkled into lively pleasure.

"Well, who do we have here?" he asked, striding toward us.

I introduced Elmer, and Dr. Corey inquired, "Does he wish to enroll in the School of Theology? We already have several here like him, you know." We laughed.

He motioned me to a chair by his desk and we quickly dispatched the matter I had come to discuss. I had pursued work through both the Theological School and the College of Liberal Arts, and this visit was to check up on required credits.

As I rose to leave, the professor said, almost diffidently, "Would you mind letting Elmer play here on my desk for a little while?"

When I placed Elmer down on the polished desk top, he promptly seized Dr. Corey's finger, looked him straight in the eye and reeled off several rapid sentences of earnest monkey talk. Then he whirled about and made a madcap dash for the pen holder.

Having anticipated this, I also lunged toward the pen, but the monkey was too fast for me. I grabbed him just as he got the green fountain pen in a tight little fist. The professor chuckled with amusement while I clung to the wriggling, shrilly objecting monkey and peeled his clutching fingers from around the pen.

"Oh, let him have it," Dr. Corey urged. I had to explain that, aside from the fact that I didn't like Elmer tampering with people's good fountain pens, he had developed a fondness for the taste of ink and sucked it greedily from every pen he could get his hands on. I doubted that this was at all good for him.

Dr. Corey agreed that ink was probably not the best thing in the world for a monkey's stomach. Then he rummaged in

his pocket and pulled out a piece of peppermint candy. "Is
it all right if I give him this?"

I assented since Dr. Corey was so kind and eager to
please Elmer. I didn't have the heart to say that I never gave
him candy.

Elmer loved that peppermint, and he loved the professor
for giving it to him. He leaned affectionately against Dr.
Corey's starched shirt cuff while he licked and smacked.
This was even better than ink! Now and then he laid a sticky
hand on that gleaming white cuff while he looked up into
the bemused eyes of the professor and crooned and
chattered. He seemed to be saying that everything in the
whole world was good because he could sit on the desk of
a nice man down at the School of Theology and suck a
peppermint candy.

All at once the class bell jangled and I sprang up,
reminded that this had been an overlong visit. I scooped
Elmer off the desk and hastily pried the candy from his
protesting fingers.

Dr. Corey said, "Wait a minute." He hurried out into the
hall and returned quickly with a Kleenex Tissue dampened
at the drinking fountain.

"You can't have him against your white blouse with
those sticky hands," he said. Then, with his silver-streaked
hair falling askew above his finely lined face, Dr. Corey
wiped the monkey's gummy little mouth and fingers.

"There, that's better," he said, giving Elmer a couple of
extra pats. He didn't seem to mind at all that there were
monkey fingerprints all over his left shirt cuff.

When I reported Dr. Corey's reactions to my psychology
professor, he rubbed his hands together in appreciation.

"Now *there's* a man who has his marbles together!" he declared. But then Dr. Yorkman's impishness got the better of him and he added, "Even theologians can be human at times."

≫ 6 ≪

Dining Out

Perhaps it was because of his smallness that I could take Elmer many places where other animals would never be allowed. I discovered this the first time we dined out, modestly, at the drugstore counter on Snider Plaza.

After a day of classes, the Plaza offered a change of pace and the chance to do a few errands before settling down for hours of study. Elmer also needed a change since he was tired and bored after hours of nothing to do except sleep, suck his thumb, spy on the neighbors, and chew on things while he waited for me to come home.

So we would sally forth with Elmer, all five inches of him not counting tail, serenely viewing the world from his refuge on my shoulder.

A ribbon leash attached to the belt around my waist was also fastened to the back of Elmer's diaper. Otherwise, he promptly undid the safety pin. Therefore the sturdy pin held both diaper and leash together.

It was during one of these jaunts on a late afternoon that I walked up to the drugstore counter and ordered a glass of pop and a cracker. While Elmer clung to a lock of my hair with one hand and munched his cracker, I stood sipping my pop.

The lady behind the counter said, "Honey, why don't you all sit down to drink your pop?"

I pointed to Elmer and told her I thought there were probably rules against animals being seated at the counter.

She laughed and said, "Oh, dogs and cats, yes. But who ever heard of a rule against a little bitty ol' monkey? Besides, he acts a lot more human than some of the characters I serve here."

So we sat down. What's more, Elmer did not stay on my shoulder. The waitress and a couple of other helpers insisted that I let him down on the counter so they could see him better.

Elmer hopped about happily, chirruping and crooning his appreciation. When someone handed him a piece of ice, he was ecstatic! He licked it, he threw it from one hand to the other, he rubbed the soles of his feet with it. He jumped up and down and tossed it in the air and caught it.

Finally, when the ice melted, Elmer peered at the cold, wet spot on the counter and scratched himself in bafflement. Someone was ready to go for another piece of ice when I scooped up my charge and said goodbye. I had work waiting.

During the walk home, I contemplated with surprise the fact that I had been allowed to sit at a lunch counter with the monkey. Not only allowed but urged! Also, I had been going to that place for two years, and not until today had I known a single thing about those waitresses—not even their names. Now they were friends, about whom I knew a great deal.

The self-effacing black woman was Lillian James, who, with her meager savings, was helping her son work his way through Princeton University. The seemingly flippant white girl, Judy Owens, went to her church early each morning to pray for her young retarded sister. These revelations were shared while we were collectively under the mysterious spell of a pert baby monkey.

"Elmer, you're a wonder," I murmured as I stroked the sleek little head nestled so confidently against my cheek.

A later experience, however, brought Elmer and me in contact with a much different individual.

When we again sat at that lunch counter on Snider Plaza, a denim-clad man swaggered up to the seat next to us. Pitching his hat onto an empty stool to his right, he yelled to the waitress, "Hey, cutie, bring me a coupla doughnuts and some black coffee."

Then he became aware of Elmer, who sat quietly in the crook of my arm munching a cracker.

Jake, as the waitress called him, at once began to guffaw and waggle his fingers at the monkey. Elmer replied with a few insolent monkey remarks, then pointedly returned to the cracker. It was plain that he disliked this person and wanted to have nothing to do with him.

This behavior only whetted Jake's interest and made him redouble his efforts to get the monkey's attention. But Elmer made it clear, to the rest of us at least, that as far as he was concerned, this man just didn't exist.

That is, not until Jake paused in frustration to console himself with a smoke. When he struck a match and lit a cigarette, the monkey's all-consuming curiosity overcame his antipathy. He couldn't take his eyes off that cigarette and the vapor pouring out of it.

Suddenly, Elmer streaked from my arm to the counter and pranced about, stretching to grab at the swirling smoke.

At one point the little monk felt certain he had caught a handful of smoke, and he carefully opened his fist to look. Puzzled, he stared long at the empty hand and scratched his ribs with the other.

Meanwhile, Jake waved his cigarette in the air and howled his raucous laughter up and down the counter.

Ignoring all the noise, Elmer now reached toward the cigarette. He had decided that if he couldn't catch the smoke, he would at least try to examine its source.

A woman who had sat down on the other side of me asked a question. I had just turned to answer her when there was a sudden high shriek of pain from Elmer.

"What happened?" I demanded as I whirled around and drew the screaming monkey to me.

Roaring with laughter, Jake punctuated the air with his cigarette while he tried to answer.

"Funniest damn thing I ever seen!" he gasped. Finally, between howling guffaws and much slapping of his sides, he said, "I offered the little cuss my cigarette, hot end first, and by golly, he took it! Lord, was that funny!"

However, Jake had the laughter all to himself. The waitress glared at him, arms folded rigidly across her chest. The scattering of customers sat silent and reproachful.

As for me, I carefully pushed back my unfinished drink and then, still cuddling the crying monkey against me, stood up ever so slowly and, without a glance at the bellowing man, took my departure.

At home, I went immediately to Mrs. Swenson to get ice cubes and a pan of water for the monkey's burned hand.

"I thought you just went to Snider Plaza," she said. "How in the world did Elmer burn his hand down there?"

After I told her the story, Mrs. Swenson's usually mild blue eyes blazed beneath her white hair. Every inch of her short frame was drawn up into a pillar of fury. "I hope you really raked that good-for-nothing brute over the coals!"

Pushing Elmer's hand deeper into the water, I replied, "No, I didn't. As a matter of fact, I just walked out without saying a word."

Mrs. Swenson gasped. "But why?"

"Well, for one thing, Elmer was screaming with pain and fright and I had to get him out of there. But also, the man was so callous and insensible that it seemed hopeless. I really wanted to lash out at him—to ask him if he didn't know that this little monkey is one of God's creatures as much as he is—that Elmer has feelings and that he hurts just like anyone else. I wanted to ask him how he'd like to have someone deliberately burn him and then laugh about it."

Mrs. Swenson responded indignantly, "You should have!"

Suddenly I knew she was right. By not speaking up I had failed Elmer and all other defenseless creatures like him.

But I'd also failed the man, Jake. It is a part of my faith that even the "Jakes" of this world are not completely hopeless. Something might have penetrated his hardness if

I had spoken. I hoped fervently that I would never again remain silent in the presence of insensitivity.

An ordinary lunch counter on Snider Plaza was one thing, a modern restaurant something else. It seemed fairly certain I'd get ordered out of one of those places if I entered with a monkey.

However, after the summer session of school ended, I headed for Iowa to visit my parents and immediately found myself in just such a dilemma. I had started late in the afternoon and driven several hours before stopping to eat. Now, here I was in front of a large, stream-lined restaurant, the only eating place I'd seen for some time, and it was doubtful when there would be another. Should I go in?

It's true I had food for Elmer, and could have given it to him and left him in his cage. But he was tired and wanted out of the car as much as I did. Also, people were forever trying to buy him, and I was afraid someone would just reach in and grab him since it was too hot to leave the car windows closed. So I decided to put Elmer in his carrying cage and take him in. They couldn't do more than throw us out.

No one seemed to pay us any attention as I strode in with attempted nonchalance and looked about for a place to sit. Finding a corner table and feeling like a criminal, I stealthily placed the cage on the chair between me and the wall. I stuck a finger into the cage and hoped that Elmer would be content to chew on it and be quiet. The cage wasn't much more than purse size, and because it was below the table level, it wouldn't be noticed—if only its occupant kept still.

But that monkey liked to see and be seen, so while the waiter took my order, Elmer, ignoring my frantically wagging finger, jumped up and down, trilled and chattered, and rattled and rocked his cage.

The waiter grew more and more distracted. His eyes strayed from his order pad to the chair beside me. Finally, with pencil poised in midair, he asked, "What have you got there?"

"Well, here goes my dinner," I told myself, as I ruefully held up the cage so that the man could see my tiny, now grinning companion.

An elfin hand reached out from between the wires in a gesture of friendship to the waiter, while two dark eyes gleamed happily from that smooth, dusky little face. I was ready to get up and leave, expecting to hear that this was against the rules.

But when I saw the man put his hand out to meet Elmer's, I began to relax. Elmer clung tightly to one of the waiter's fingers, and monkey and man grinned at each other.

Before long most of the workers in the establishment had gathered around us. My waiter picked up the small cage and placed it firmly on top of the table. "Hope you don't mind," he said. "We'd all like to enjoy this little guy."

Thereafter, both the dining room help and the diners joined in a state of camaraderie and tender hilarity—or whatever it is that happens to a roomful of people in the presence of an animated, doll-sized monkey.

Elmer ate leisurely while directing his attention first to one person and then to another. Holding his bit of bread or carrot in one hand, he would either swing by the other hand, or else reach out to touch anyone going by. Sometimes, in an extra spurt of exuberance, he dropped everything to stand on his head or swing by his tail.

His crowning act, however, came after I ordered milk for his doll bottle. He sat back on his heels, held the bottle up and smacked down its contents. His audience howled with glee. When the bottle was empty, Elmer jerked off the nipple, peered inside, then poked a string-sized finger in to be certain that all the milk was gone.

But instead of tossing the bottle aside as he always did at home, he held it out to the waiter for more milk.

Thus, Elmer's bottle was filled again and again, all on the house.

By now the monkey was out of his cage and on my table, since everyone, after that first bottle of milk, had clamored for him to be taken out so they could see him better. Behind his upheld bottle, Elmer's bright eyes constantly roved over the admiring audience to see if everyone was enjoying his act. He was having as much fun as they were.

However, I was watching that little belly grow rounder and tighter by the minute. For the sake of such applause, that little showoff seemed ready to keep right on taking milk until he exploded like an over-inflated balloon.

I called a halt.

As we took our leave, Elmer sat on my shoulder and whistled and trilled to all his new-found friends. They responded in turn with a unity of lilting voices, "Goodbye, Elmer! Goodbye, Elmer!"

I paused just outside the door and looked back. A short time before, that entire roomful of people had been cooly dignified and solitary. Now they were relaxed and laughing, and everyone seemed to be speaking to everyone else.

I marveled at the change, and we continued on our journey.

We arrived at my parents' home in Iowa the next day. Here again Elmer did not lack for attention. He constantly chirruped and trilled his appreciation for the choice morsels of food presented him by my father and mother, and then by numerous nieces and nephews, who soon showed up in full force.

These small fry, by the way, promptly began to call the monkey "Cousin Elmer," and me "our favorite Aunt." One look at that lively little ball of fur with the shiny eyes and big grin, and I, his foster mother, promptly shot to great heights in their estimation. It was almost impossible to refuse, therefore, when an eager little girl or boy put loving arms around my neck and whispered in my ear, "Aunt Gertrude, may I give Elmer his bottle this time?"

My son Ross joined me at my parents' home. He and Glen had spent the summer out west. Glen stayed there to attend the University of Washington. Ross planned to travel with me back to Southern Methodist University by way of Chicago.

The Chicago trip would give us the opportunity to spend some time with a young married couple, Fran and Jerrome, and a bachelor friend. The three had been my sons' traveling companions when they were all struggling eastward across the snowy mountains at the southern tip of South America. The friendship had continued and Fran and Jerrome had been our recent guests in Dallas.

At the time Ross and Glen met the bachelor, he was an avowed monkey hater. He was also hairy and bearded, and declared he wasn't going to shave until he got out of that gosh-awful country.

So naturally, when Ross and Glen acquired their hairy black baby, he reminded them of their friend and they gleefully christened the monkey "Elmer."

"Big Elmer" was not exactly flattered.

Soon after our arrival in Chicago, our friends obtained reservations at a rather posh restaurant. I did not plan to take the monkey since I was certain he would not be admitted.

But just as we were ready to leave, we had a problem. Elmer, squalling his frantic little-baby squalls, followed my every move with terror-stricken eyes. He was a nervous wreck and getting worse by the minute. He knew, as always, when he was going to be left behind.

And now, to make matters infinitely worse, here he was in a strange house with a big barking dog and a lusty, talkative parrot. In addition, a shrunken head from Ecuador stared down from the wall.

I don't suppose the shrunken head bothered the monkey much, but the loud dog did; and so did the parrot, even though he, like Elmer, came from Brazil. In the mornings the parrot strutted around, impatiently demanding his coffee in Portuguese. But the language of Elmer's native land by no means soothed the little monk. After the parrot had guzzled all the coffee he wanted, he spent the rest of the day putting his acquired North American culture to use. He swore eloquently in English.

The whole thing was just too much for Elmer. He was in a frenzy of despair.

Fran and Jerrome settled it when they said, "We'll take him with us!"

"But they'll kick us out, won't they?" Ross asked.

"Nah," Jerrome replied. "We'll smuggle him in."

"And besides," added Fran, "what harm can a clean little caged monkey do?"

The carpeting in the restaurant was lush beneath our feet. Overhead, the chandeliers winked in subdued elegance. No one noticed that what I carried at my side was not a handbag.

No one would have a chance to notice, anyway, for my friends surrounded me and talked animatedly while we were shown to our table. Though Big Elmer carefully walked on the opposite side from the monkey, he did contribute his share to the conversational cover-up.

As we were being seated, I surreptitiously placed the cage under the table and poked a cracker in, hoping intensely this would keep the monkey quiet. I felt somewhat guilty, but my young friends were enjoying the subterfuge, so I concluded I might as well relax and enjoy it with them.

As long as Big Elmer didn't have to sit next to or touch Little Elmer, he didn't seem to mind the monkey's presence. Little Elmer, however, was not so cooperative. He was decidedly averse to a seating arrangement that kept him down in the dark with only shuffling feet for company. No mere cracker would make up for the world of laughing people and soft lights above that table.

He promptly began to make his feelings known.

He started out politely enough as the white-coated waiter took our orders. Fran and I ordered lamb chops while the men carried on a rather high-pitched conversation about digging their way through the snows of Southern Chile. Then, while the men gave their orders, Fran and I lifted our voices on another subject.

The conversations at other tables and the background music also helped us, but above it all, Little Elmer chirruped periodic questions that cut sharply through the human hubbub. Our suave waiter attended meticulously to each order, but his dark countenance had taken on a preoccupied air, and his ears seemed to stand out with listening.

Finally, when all orders were taken, he paused to ask, "Have you folks been hearing some strange noises?"

Mercifully, Little Elmer was silent for the moment. Ross and our friends shrugged, spread their hands, and looked up at him with blank faces.

By the time the waiter had returned with the salads, however, Elmer's patience was wearing thin. His mannerly, questioning tones turned into shrieks that grew progressively louder and could not be drowned out by any amount of music, talk and dining activity.

Our waiter stood with the tray of salads poised delicately on one hand and asked reproachfully, "What do you folks have under this table?"

My friends exchanged wry, caught-in-the-act grins while I dragged the small cage out from under the table.

"I'm really sorry," I told the waiter. "We had hoped this little rascal would keep quiet and give no trouble." Then I told the others to go ahead with their dinner while I took the monkey to the car.

"Wait a moment," said the waiter. A wide smile lit up his grave features. He had everyone move over just a little and placed an extra chair next to me. Then talking to Elmer gently, he picked up the caged monkey and placed him on the chair.

"I'm sure this little fellow will be quiet now," he told us. "He was just lonesome down on the floor."

The waiter was right. Little Elmer now became a well-behaved dinner companion. Perhaps he automatically responded to the soft lights and plush surroundings. During the entire evening of music, singing and dining, he alternately sucked his thumb and ate, taking time out for some serious monkey talk to the waiter each time he came by, and trilling softly over all the small delicacies the man brought him.

Once again, dinner was enhanced by the presence of this small monkey working his magic. Even Big Elmer bore up under the presence of his namesake, although each time the waiter came along with some tidbit for Little Elmer, Big Elmer shuddered and groaned. After all, a monkey-hater had his reputation to uphold.

Elmer's dining out was not restricted to public places. We were often invited to the homes of friends though I never took him unless his company had been specifically requested.

At such times I brought his larger cage along, put in toys for him to play with, then gave him his dinner in the cage while the rest of us sat at the table. There were occasions, however, when it didn't work out this way.

About two years after the Chicago incident, while I was serving as a parish minister, Betty Jackson invited Elmer and me to her house for dinner. She wanted it to be a cozy little affair with just herself, her husband, the monkey and me.

I knew that Betty and her husband were having trouble and that there was rumor of divorce. I had a strong suspicion Betty felt that since I was her minister, I could just wave a heavenly wand and make things right again for the two of them. I had no such confidence in myself, much as I yearned to be of help.

Things got off to a bad start. It was chilly and Elmer could never stand cold weather without being clothed. He shook and trembled and gasped when taken out into the cold without something on. He even had to wear a shirt and undershirt in the house on especially cold days, and this was one of those days.

Worse, knowing Betty's husband, I hadn't wanted to bring Elmer.

Bradley Jackson prided himself on being a rough, tough, self-made man. He had accumulated his thousands—some said millions—in the lumber industry. I could well imagine what he would have to say about a female who had nothing more to do with her time than play dress-up with a monkey and make inane speeches on Sunday mornings. It was bad enough for him to know I was a minister, without having to show up with a monkey in shirt and pants.

Bradley was in another part of the house when I arrived, so I quickly put the monkey's cage in a far corner, shoved Elmer into it, and closed the door.

Betty and I visited as she bustled about her kitchen. I helped where I could and soon there was a sumptuous meal on the table.

Betty seemed at the point of calling her husband. Instead, she said, "Now, we'll get Elmer up to the table."

Overriding my vigorous remonstrations, she produced a high chair and ordered me to get Elmer out of the cage. She got him a small plate and even tied a bib under his chin. Then, seeing that he couldn't reach his tray, Betty got a dictionary to elevate him to the proper height. By the time her husband was called onto the scene, the enthroned Elmer was grinning broadly, and I was fervently wishing that I could drop through the floor.

Bradley greeted me with icy politeness, and the look he gave that little red-shirted monkey seemed to be one of pure contempt.

Bradley Jackson's cold attitude literally filled the room. There was a sense of darkness about us, even though the winter sun streamed brightly through the window. Betty and I, who had talked pleasantly while preparing the meal, now found our conversation stifled by this brooding presence.

The roast, the baked potatoes, the lovely green salad, and the homemade rolls were passed in almost total silence. I tried hard to make a few cheerful remarks about Betty's fine cooking, but the cheer part didn't come off very well. Betty murmured a wilted "thank-you" or two, while her husband stared at his plate and ate in utter silence.

I dug about desperately in my mind for something to say to Bradley—for anything that would force him to look up and say a word or two. But that wall of iciness seemed impregnable.

The only one not subdued by Bradley's attitude was Elmer. He had eaten most of his meal in the cage and now merely toyed with a crusty roll.

Ignoring both Betty and me, he gave his real attention to our host and monkey-talked constantly to the dour man across the table. At long last, after his chatter had failed to bring even a flicker of response, Elmer cocked his head first to one side, then to the other, and scrutinized that man most intently. This was something new under the sun—a human being that gave him, Elmer, absolutely no attention.

Through all of this I tried discretely to divert Elmer and silence him. Once I half-rose, intending to put the monkey back in his cage, but Betty caught my eye and shook her head.

To my surprise, Elmer actually seemed to like our uncommunicative host. The monkey was capable of taking a great dislike to an individual and when that happened, Elmer was the one who refused to communicate.

Not so now.

Since Bradley disdained to notice him, Elmer merely changed his tactics. After a few head-tipping observations, he puckered his mouth into a small "o" and emitted shattering cascades of trills and whistles.

Still no recognition from across the table.

At this point, Elmer stopped and scratched industriously, as he always did when trying to figure something out. I relaxed slightly, thinking that at last this mortifying little pest had given up and would keep quiet.

How mistaken I was!

Seconds later, I looked up to see him rolling something swiftly between his hands. Horrified, I realized he was making spit balls from the soft insides of his dinner roll.

My fork halted in midair as Elmer, with devilish glee, sprang upright and aimed a wad of dough straight across the table at our host. It hit Bradley square in the face! In split-second succession and with unerring accuracy, another followed, and another and another.

Doing a bit of fast armwork myself, I grabbed that grinning little rascal out of his high chair and away from his ammunition. Elmer wriggled and kicked like all possessed while I clamped him in my hands and waited for the sky to fall.

Bradley Jackson was coughing into his napkin and wiping his face and eyes. When he finally lifted his head, I saw in astonishment that he was laughing.

He looked at Elmer and said, "Why, you damned little devil!"

Then, seeming to think this was not quite the proper thing to say in front of the minister, he floundered about for a way to express himself more politely.

I said, "That's all right, Mr. Jackson. This monkey often affects me the same way. I'm ashamed of him and I'll shut him in his cage right now."

But Bradley objected vigorously. "Oh, no, let him stay, by all means. Why, he and I are just getting acquainted. By the way, where'd you get the damned little—I mean—well, where'd you get him?"

The ice was broken at last. Elmer was giddy with happiness, now that everyone was laughing and talking. Then, since things were going so well, he impishly took one more liberty. As Betty passed me the sugar for my coffee, Elmer took a lightning dive as it went by and came up with a fistful of sugar. This, too, delighted our host, but since he was now on his best behavior and couldn't use his most descriptive phrases, he only chuckled. Then he looked straight at Betty and winked.

I'd like to think that Elmer saved this marriage, but I'm pretty certain that would not be true. I do believe, however, that on that particular day he did break down a most formidable barrier of non-communication between a husband and wife.

⇒ 7 ⇐

Babies Together

Elmer's vast curiosity, love of fun, and quick intelligence were evident from the beginning. His response to my efforts to housebreak him was typical of his intelligence. At appropriate times I put my simian baby on a newspaper on the floor and told him what he was supposed to do. He immediately grasped the idea.

Shortly after this toilet training began, we visited my sister Dessie and her family. The monkey had been playing happily with the two smaller children when he suddenly stopped and began to look about. A book lay open on the floor but he saw no newspaper. Well, that book was paper, wasn't it? Four-year-old Kerry and his one-year-old sister Karen looked on gravely while their tiny companion climbed daintily onto the open book and puddled on its pages.

Unfortunately, Elmer's toilet training could not be completely successful for two reasons. One was that he had to be left in his cage for long periods of time, first while I attended school, and later while I served as parish minister.

The second reason was his excitable nature. With the right provocation, Elmer shot into an excess of joy, fear, or rage. In the throes of any of these emotions he lost all control of himself and became a bouncing leaky faucet. Nevertheless, as soon as the excitement died down, the monkey's presence of mind reasserted itself. Seeing those puddles, he dashed for the Kleenex and industriously set to work mopping up. He had early observed that this was the proper procedure. Naturally he cast a quick eye over his shoulder now and then to see whether those present understood what a superb "mopper-upper" he was.

Elmer and my sister's family delighted in each other. In addition to their two smaller children, Dessie and her husband Jack had a boy and girl in grade school.

Another important member of the family was Mehitabel the cat. Though just an ordinary-sized cat, she was still several times larger than the monkey and regarded him with tolerant superiority. Even so, she was never able to resist his invitation to a game of hide and seek.

Elmer, a small streak of mischief, dashed up and tapped the cat smartly, then tore off with lightening speed. Mehitabel, no slouch herself at speed, took off after him. However, she couldn't keep up with him, and she couldn't even see where he went.

She searched and searched until she finally found the monkey, who invariably sat on top of a lamp, a window, or a door, and grinned down at her. When she located Elmer on top of the kitchen door, Mehitabel struggled valiantly to climb the slick surface to reach him. To no avail. It was triumph for the monk, humiliation for the cat, and great enjoyment for the children.

Small Karen and the monkey were especially interested in each other. Karen toddled after Elmer and periodically slapped at him or gingerly ran her hand through his black hair. Sometimes she even pulled him by the tail, and the young monkey endured treatment from her that he would not have taken from anyone else without protest. It was as though he understood that she also was just a baby.

These two were fascinated by each other's bottles. Karen stole and sampled Elmer's every chance she got, while the monkey seized Karen's any time she dropped it. He wrapped his legs and arms and tail around it, got his mouth over the nipple, and sucked away blissfully. Actually, it wasn't always necessary to swipe bottles since either baby, without the intervention of big folks, would exchange bottles obligingly.

Karen and the monkey also shared other things, like Elmer's Sugar Pops. As a special treat, I sometimes put a few Sugar Pops into a small bottle, screwed the cap on securely and gave it to the monkey. This provided him with boundless delight. After he shook the bottle and watched the pops roll about to his heart's content, he then set to work unscrewing the cap. It was a challenge he loved. No matter how tight the cap was, he eventually got it off. Then came the really good part. His small fingers dug for the Pops, one at a time, and each was eaten with great relish.

One day little Karen stood by open-mouthed, wistfully observing him. Elmer glanced up and saw her. With a Sugar Pop halfway to his mouth, he swiftly reversed the motion and popped it into Karen's mouth instead.

The next time I prepared a bottle of treats for the monkey
I fixed one for Karen. As it turned out, she could not get the
cap off her bottle so Elmer happily undid it for her. Not to
be left out, four-year-old Kerry also asked for Sugar Pops,
and he also wanted the monkey to open his bottle.

Elmer had two loves that Kerry and Karen could not
easily share: soap and green onions. One day Dessie skidded
into the bathroom over a slick floor to find her small
progenies tearfully gagging and foaming at the mouth.

"What's the matter?" she demanded.

For answer Karen pointed a pudgy finger at her mouth
while Kerry said, with tearful conviction, "Soap don't taste
good!"

"Why were you eating soap?" Dessie asked.

Kerry pointed an accusing finger at the monkey. "He
started it!"

Sure enough, there on the top of the washbowl sat the
instigator of the crime, smacking blissfully over a bar of
soap.

While Dessie and I rinsed off kids, monkey and floor,
we agreed that this had to be the most sanitary monkey in
all existence. Not only was he kept spotless on the outside,
but with all that soap he must be squeaky clean on the inside.

Perhaps it was because of their unhappy experience with
soap that the children, as far as I knew, never tried anointing
themselves with onion juice, though they watched with
intense interest while Elmer did it.

The monkey bit his onion just enough to make the juice
run and then rubbed his whole body with the potent fluid.
Not a single spot was missed. Although he sniffled and his
eyes watered, he kept on biting and rubbing till the task was

done. For once, he was too absorbed to notice his audience. Some instinct seemed to overpower him with an urge for onion juice. Perhaps it served as a much-needed personal hygiene. Once through with his onion ritual, Elmer was again alert to his whole environment and eager for more play with the children.

One of the things Elmer especially liked was to have Kerry tickle his stomach. While Kerry tickled gently, the monkey doubled up, rolled, laughed, and gave every indication of huge enjoyment. He could easily have run away if he hadn't liked it, but he never did.

The two older children, Butch and Jan, patiently awaited their turn for Elmer's attention. This came after the cat had tired of hide and seek and the two little children had been told to let the monkey rest.

The older ones then either sat or lay flat on their backs on the floor while Elmer studied them with the concentration of an eye-ear-nose-and-throat specialist. Eyebrows and eye lashes were examined, the shape of each ear was noted, and an exploratory finger poked inside. Lips were gone over with a tiny, delicate hand, while wispy, agile fingers felt each tooth separately. Even the children's pink tongues were grasped and pulled this way and that while the monkey peered gravely down their throats.

Both children would have objected to the high heavens had their parents suggested a doctor's examination, yet such was their love for this mite of a monkey that they happily remained immobile for any length of time and submitted to any kind of treatment he chose to administer.

Even away from the stimulus of the children and their cat, Elmer's learning went on. For example, from his cage near the window, he became deeply interested in the neighbor's barking dog. Elmer then began to practice barking. He became good at it too, and gave a remarkable minor key rendition of Bozo's tones. But like Bozo, Elmer barked only at appropriate times—when people were passing by.

Outside his cage, he found endless things to explore. He loved to crawl under the spread on my daybed and, giddy with adventure, race wildly up and down, back and forth. Visitors were often mystified at that jumping bed cover, until I dug out the grinning, wiggly monk.

A closed drawer was a challenge to Elmer's ingenuity. He used a pencil, ruler or any other stick-like object at hand to try to pry it open. He usually succeeded too, if there was the smallest chink for him to get his pry into.

I marveled not only at his smartness, but at his strength, considering his feather-lightness. He braced his legs and pulled back mightily with his hands on the lever. After all that effort I found it hard to reprimand the little rascal when he gleefully began to drag out the contents of the drawer. Often times he had a drawer open before I knew what was up. More than once I glanced away from my studies to see a white blouse flutter madly across the floor with two mischievous eyes agleam beneath it.

For Elmer, along with Kerry and Karen, every waking moment brought new experiences, new learning, new skills. Unlike the children, the monkey would never be able to talk. He communicated extremely well, though, by means of certain sounds and gestures.

Elmer held his own with the other two at this time, and in some ways almost outdistanced them, as in his use of a tool. But the three little ones, playing happily, appeared to give no thought to their differences. They were just babies together.

≫ 8 ≪

Jericho Road

Travel with a young monkey is just about like taking a trip with a human baby. It involves extra time and effort and I had little of either to spare when I left Dallas, Texas, at 6:15 on the evening of June 10th, 1955.

I had just completed my schooling and was due three days and two thousand miles later at Walla Walla, Washington, site of my church's Annual Conference.

I could just about make it on time if I drove fast, put in long hours, and didn't make too many stops. This presupposed that both Elmer and my car would cooperate to the fullest.

The four-year-old Ford had just been tuned up and serviced by an outfit that charged a stiff fee and assured me that everything was in perfect running order. I knew Elmer was in good running order. My challenge now was to keep the car running and the monkey sitting.

Books occupied most of the trunk and the inside space from the floor to seat level. My other things were crammed in wherever a bit of room could be found. Elmer's big cage, packed full, sat in the back seat, while his smaller cage sat atop a suitcase beside me in front. This gave him a comfortably high vantage point from which to view the world.

I said goodbye to my gently disapproving friends, who thought a woman had no business taking off on such a long trip alone, especially at night. Then Elmer and I climbed into the weighted down car and headed west.

As we moved through the city with the stream of evening traffic, I reassured myself that my friends' fears were groundless. After all, this wasn't the first time I'd made this journey and I'd never had any trouble before. All I had to do was sit in the car and drive—and stop occasionally to eat or give Elmer a bit of exercise. It was good to know that the car was in such fine shape.

The monkey rode in his cage that evening but he didn't mind, especially since he could watch several miles of bright lights and people on our way out of Dallas. What's more, each time we halted for a traffic light, he could jump up and down in the window to attract waves, yells and smiles from the occupants of other cars. All this was fun for me as well as for Elmer.

Long before we were even out of the city, however, I became concerned about my "in perfect running order" Ford. It was vibrating most peculiarly. At first, I wasn't sure who had the shakes—me or the car. For some time I had been working hard under considerable pressure.

In fact, I was still under pressure for I *had* to get to this Conference. Among other things, I needed to be there ahead of time to prepare for my ordination. Also, I was to be interviewed and appointed to a local church in Eastern Washington which I would begin serving immediately after the conference. Before beginning work, though, I would have to hurry to my home on the coast, pack and arrange to have my furniture moved.

All this had been going through my mind when I became aware of that vibration. It seemed to run from the steering wheel through my fingertips, clear down to my toes. Was it I or the car? I finally decided that no matter how shaky I might be, this car had the shakes also!

Once we were out of the heaviest traffic, I stopped at a filling station to have the car examined. It appeared to me that the mechanic gave the monkey more attention than the car. He declared that he had inspected the auto carefully and couldn't find a single thing wrong. He looked at me as though I was a mere woman who didn't know anything about an automobile. Which I was, and didn't. But when he suggested I was imagining things, that was another matter. I thanked him politely and went on. There seemed to be no other choice.

As long as I drove at a fast speed, the shivering vibration was not noticeable. But whenever I slowed down for traffic or rough roads, then again my Ford did the Shimmies. At such times I hung grimly onto the wheel while Elmer clutched the bars of his cage, and his dark eyes flared in alarm.

Later that evening, at a gasoline station in a small town, I asked the attendant if he would please drive my car around to see how it acted and tell me what was wrong. He obligingly climbed in beside the protesting monkey and drove off, while I stood and waited. There was no room for another person in the loaded vehicle.

Upon his return, he declared, "Well, there's nothing wrong with your car, aside from a noisy monkey. It runs perfectly."

He lectured me about a woman going on a long trip alone, then challenged, "But lady, if you're determined to make this trip, stop worrying and get rolling!"

What else could I do? I didn't exactly stop worrying, but I did get rolling and put a good many miles behind me before stopping for the night.

Early morning found Elmer and me bathed, packed into the car, and shimmying west across the Texas Plains. Again, the car drove much better as it picked up speed. Still, whenever I stopped for gas I told my story of the vibrating car. Each time, someone looked under the hood, tinkered for awhile, then came around to shake hands and laugh with the monkey while assuring me that the Ford was fine and there was nothing to worry about.

By the time we stopped that second night, we were out of Texas and nearly half-way across New Mexico. The next morning we passed through Albuquerque then angled northwest. I stopped for gas and again voiced my concern about the vibration.

This time there was a different reaction. The mechanic yelled from under the hood, "I've found your problem!" Then he did some adjusting and told me he had it all fixed and I'd have no more trouble.

Well, the road was good, the desert was hot, and I had to get to that Conference. Elmer whimpered drearily. He was tired of the heat and the scenery. I stepped on the gas and held the speedometer at eighty though I was still not thoroughly convinced that all was well.

At noon we were nearing the southwest corner of Colorado. Elmer had ridden most of the morning on my shoulder but was now back in his cage. The road rose and fell under the hot sun while the Ford ate up the miles. I had almost forgotten my worries.

Then an odd thing happened. A huge insect of some sort splatted messily against the windshield. As I sped over the brow of a long, steep hill, I saw a graveled place beside the road with room enough to pull over and park.

I got out and began to clean the glass while I told myself ruefully that this was a foolish waste of precious time. My view of the road had not been hampered. It was just that I couldn't stand the sight of that smeary, yellow-red splotch.

Elmer, glad for the change, monkey-talked companionably while I rapidly finished cleaning the windshield and got back into the car.

But when I started the Ford again, to my horror I found that I had no control over it. The steering wheel was useless under my hands. Regardless of which way I turned it, nothing happened—except that the car kept moving under its own momentum, a momentum greatly increased by the load of books. Frantically, I turned off the ignition, but the car continued on its resolute downward course.

As I breathed a hurried prayer for help, I was acutely aware of those sheer drop-offs at both sides of the road, and of the lonely sage dotted desert below. All thoughts of the Conference that had previously pressed so urgently upon my mind were blotted out. Instead, the images of my three sons swam before me. From my heart I telegraphed them my love. How hard it would be if they were to loose their mother so soon after the death of their father.

While my inner being reached for divine intervention, I continued to twist the unresponsive steering wheel. I had no idea what would happen if I tried the brakes. But the road curved ahead. No way would the car negotiate that curve.

So I stepped on the brake pedal.

The Ford took a sudden terrifying swerve to the left and headed for the precipice!

Instinctively I threw my right arm against Elmer's cage to steady it for the plunge to the rocks and sage below. The car hurtled forward!

And then—it stopped! Stopped just as though some powerful force had laid a mighty hand against it!

The car's nose was even with the edge of the embankment. I sat there, stunned and still, afraid to move for fear the least tremor would put the car into motion again. Elmer chattered excitedly as he looked out over the cliff and disliked what he saw.

I had slowly begun to breathe again when I glanced toward the brow of the hill and was terrified anew!

Any car coming fast over that crest would almost certainly smash into us. Moving swiftly but carefully, I took Elmer from his cage and got out of there.

With the wind snapping my skirt and the monkey glued around my neck, I ran to the top of the hill to flag down traffic. Elmer didn't like the wind and had absorbed my fear; I could tell by the feel of him and the sound of his whimpers.

Traffic was sparse on this desert highway, but soon a long, shiny Cadillac slid to a halt beside us. A well dressed man and woman stepped from the car and walked downhill with us to survey our predicament.

How they did it remains a mystery to me, but while Elmer and I guarded the top of the hill, the couple managed to get my heavily loaded car off the road and back onto the narrow right shoulder. They put stones under the wheels to prevent it from rolling.

My benefactors told me to get in with them and they would take me to the next town where I could get help. I put a bottle and a few other things for Elmer in my purse, then put Elmer on my shoulder and locked the Ford.

The woman asked, "Don't you think you should just leave the monkey in the car?"

Leave Elmer? I stood there speechless.

She saw my shocked look and relented. I suppose she had visions of him running all over their beautiful Cadillac, getting into the Kleenex, the ash trays, and tinkering with knobs and dials. Elmer might well have done all this except that his leash was anchored securely to my belt. So he rode the next sixty miles to Cortez, Colorado, on my lap or shoulder.

Elmer didn't seem to mind that he couldn't do anything but talk, for he was in a conversational mood. As usual, after any time of fright, he comforted himself with a stream of soothing chatter. Most of the way to Cortez his crooning tones told us that now everything was okay and we didn't have to be afraid any more.

Our new friends also talked. Their names, they told me, were Steward and Jessica Wellington and they were from

Albuquerque. Steward drove with an expert, careless ease and his wife sat straight and graceful. She, a slender brunette, wore clothes that subtly and smoothly complimented her fine shades of skin and body curves. He, a tall, broad-shouldered blond, would have made a superb model for men's fashions.

I discovered to my surprise that this impeccably groomed couple were on their way to prospect for uranium in the mountains of Colorado. I wondered if they would look equally suave in their prospecting clothes, which must have been stashed away in the trunk, for there wasn't the slightest hint of such outdoor activity in the gleaming, uncluttered interior of their car.

By the time we reached the outskirts of Cortez, Elmer was trilling his usual happy mood. Then, in sudden exuberance, he sprang from my lap to the silken shoulder of Mrs. Wellington. I reached quickly to take him back, but this woman who an hour before had suggested leaving him in the stalled Ford, now put her hand up and held him against her cheek.

She said softly, "We're just fine. Let him stay."

From then on into town, the monkey blissfully alternated between grooming Jessica's coif of dark hair and examining her blue earrings. By the time we finally located a garage where I could get help, both Mrs. Wellington and her husband were deeply absorbed in the antics of the monkey. When Elmer and I left the car, they were pleased by his reluctance to part from them.

I tried to get these Good Samaritans to accept some remuneration for all their bother. They shrugged it off lightly by saying anybody would have done the same. I was not at all certain about that but contented myself with taking down their address. A letter of appreciation would be sent later.

Before driving away they admonished me cheerfully, "Now don't have any more car wrecks, and take good care of Elmer!"

I sat in the shabby garage and waited for someone to find the time to tow my car in. Since it was Sunday, this was the sole garage we had found open, and there were only one or two people around. The gas pump attendant grinned and whistled at Elmer while he worked, and Elmer grinned and whistled right back. This was much to his liking but not especially to mine. Time was wasting.

At last, a rusty tow truck rattled around the corner. Elmer and I climbed in beside the driver. We banged and lurched back over the same sixty miles we had earlier taken in such style. The truck shook even worse than the Ford, but in a more reassuring way, for me at least. Elmer was apprehensive about this noisy contraption. He hung on tight around my neck and after each particularly hard jolt, gave the driver a sound piece of his mind.

When we reached my car, the mechanic made a brief investigation under the hood. Then he straightened up slowly and spoke to me in an awed voice, "My God, lady, you're lucky to be alive! Your steering column's broke clean in two!"

He mopped his face with a red handkerchief and added, "If you hadn't stopped right when you did, you'd certainly have gone over the bank and tumbled out across that desert! How fast did you say you'd been driving?"

When I told him I'd been driving for a long time at around eighty, he emitted a long, slow whistle and shook his

head. Then he hitched the car to his tow truck, and all during
the drive back to town, he continued intermittently to shake
his head and marvel that I was alive.

At the garage, I was told regretfully that since this was
Sunday, they couldn't possibly have my car ready until late
the next morning. The tow truck driver, a kindly person, took
Elmer and me to the only motel vacancy in town, a dark little
room where we could stay until he came for us the next day.

Our accommodations fell short of the ideal as a place to
rest and relax. In addition, it had clouded over outside and
soon began to rain, so we couldn't even go for a walk. It was
a dreary time of waiting for me. The only bright thing in all
this was Elmer. He chirped, whistled, ran about, climbed and
explored. It was a happy respite for him. He didn't mind that
the room was dark and dusty, and that I had to wash his hands
and feet each time he wanted to be held.

It was nearly noon the next day before we got away from
Cortez. The garage mechanic had put in a new steering
column. The manager said they had looked the car over
carefully and everything was in "A-1" condition. I should
have no more trouble. That was good news. Perhaps now I
could make up for some of the time I had lost, though of
course I would still arrive late at the Conference.

In spite of my narrow escape the day before, my natural
confidence grew with each mile. No more shimmying and
shaking. As my spirits grew, so did my speed. However, by
mid-afternoon, with the sun boiling down and Elmer
traveling nude in his cage, my mood had wilted somewhat.
Elmer sucked a warm drink from his water container and
murmured complaints. He wanted to stop. I felt sorry for

him but kept my foot on the gas. I had hoped to get to Walla Walla sometime that night but the hope now faded. Though we were both suffering discomfort, Elmer could do something about his. He stretched out and went to sleep and did not fully awaken until the sun splashed low against the western horizon and the air was turning cool.

Soon we neared the section of highway that seemed to climb straight toward the sky to Soldiers Summit. Elmer shivered and whimpered with the cold so I pulled over to clothe and feed him before starting the climb. He clung to me and wanted to ride on my shoulder, but I put him back in the cage, promising him he could get out just as soon as we reached the summit.

As we started the ascent, the Ford jerked, coughed, and then died.

I tried despairingly to get it started but the motor simply refused to cooperate. I couldn't believe it!

With great effort I rolled the car backwards onto the narrow shoulder of the road, then climbed out, hoping someone would stop to help. I opened the hood but my untrained eyes could find nothing wrong.

I tried without success to flag drivers down, but one car after another roared past me and on toward the summit. The drivers eyed the road ahead and seemed not to care that their dust and gravel showered a woman in distress. They were probably hurrying home to dinner, or perhaps they didn't want to stop in all that traffic on a precarious mountain road. I couldn't really blame them.

The sun was going down fast and I was on the edge of panic. Nevertheless, I reached through the open window to hold Elmer's hand and reassure him.

As usual, in spite of any brave show I might stage, the monkey was not fooled. He absorbed my emotions and now whimpered and cried.

I contemplated getting into the car and staying there until morning, but we were so near the margin of the road that I was afraid of getting hit. Elmer's whimpering soon rose to the squalling of a frightened child, and I stood there and thought how easy it would be to join him.

At that moment I heard a car chug to a halt behind me. Pushing the windblown hair from my eyes, I turned to see a beat-up old jalopy a few yards below. It was stopped on an equally precarious rim of the road. Ragged children and a yellow dog stared out solemnly from among crammed-in household items. In the front seat was a woman whose hair fell in tired wisps about her unsmiling face. The driver, however, jumped out jauntily, tucked his wrinkled shirt into battered pants and started toward me.

"Whatsa matter there?" he yelled cheerfully.

I could have hugged every one of them, including the dog.

Instead, I explained the inability of my Ford to climb the mountain. The man promptly set to work under the hood, adjusting things here and there. As he worked, he talked. "Riley's my name, George Riley."

By way of reassurance, he added, "I used to work at the Ford plant in Detroit. I know Fords from the inside out."

Soon he finished, closed the hood, and said, "Now, lady, if you can drive my car, I can get this here rig of yours to the top of the mountain. That is, if I don't get too much backtalk out of your passenger there."

So we climbed that mountain, with me driving the rickety old car filled with the Riley household, and Mr. Riley driving my loaded down car with the caged monkey at his side.

George's wife and children were shy and quiet during the early part of our journey. The smallest one, on his mother's lap, stared at me with unwavering solemnity, and I sensed an equally intense scrutiny from the other three children in the back seat. The yellow dog, not one to stand on ceremony, took a few tentative slurps at the back of my neck.

As soon as I felt sufficiently familiar with the operation of their car, which, though old and creaky, certainly ran better than mine, I asked where they were going.

Mrs. Riley replied in a voice weighted with fatigue, "We've come all the way from Indiana, and we're headin' for the west coast of Washington. Seems like it's takin' forever."

Then she added that her husband was looking for a job there. "He wants to go to one of them places where he can do landscapin' and work with gardens and flowers and mow grass."

There wasn't a peep out of the children until I said I'd like to know their names. I began with the one on his mother's lap. "What's your name?"

He remained unblinking and solemn but there was a sudden eruption from the back seat.

"His name's Bobo," they yelled in unison.

"An' he's three years old," a young girl's voice informed me.

"An' the cat's got his tongue," announced a gruff little boy's voice, while another little girl giggled.

The children sat perched among tattered quilts and pillows and cheer bubbled out of them. I felt cheered too, even though that Conference was going on without me, and the Ford was letting me down again.

The girl on the right said her name was Lucy and she was "seven-goin'-on-eight." The boy in the middle said he was Joseph and "six-goin'-on-seven." The little girl on the left was Alice and she was "five-goin'-on-six."

I asked the name of their dog and they all yelled at once, "His name's Harry Truman!"

Watching in the rear view mirror, I saw Harry Truman jostle Alice and Joseph at the sound of his name, sit erect, and scratch himself. Then, seeming to feel that something more was required of him, he lurched forward and gave me another big slurp across my neck.

"Harry Truman, you stop that! That ain't nice!" admonished Lucy in an important, grown-up tone.

Now that the amenities had been observed, and we were all on friendly terms, the children eagerly put questions to me.

Joseph asked, "What's that we saw jumpin' around in your car? A kitten?"

When I replied, "A monkey," there was a moment of silence, and then popping excitement. They pelted me with questions about Elmer. Even solemn Bobo caught the mood and chattered.

In the midst of it all, the mother, who had been gravely staring ahead into the growing darkness, suddenly spoke.

"Children, if you watch, you can get a better look at the monkey in the car lights coming down the hill."

From then on, the children leaned forward and squealed with delight each time they thought they saw Elmer.

There was plenty of room to park at the summit. We drew up side by side in a brightly illuminated lookout area across the highway from a filling station.

As George got out of my car, he told me cheerfully, "Me and Elmer, we don't get along too well."

Elmer had protested loudly all the way, and no wonder. Having a total stranger drive off with him and the car without his "mother" was a scary experience.

The family in the other car poured out to get a look at the monkey. Since Elmer now had me and this audience, his mood promptly improved. Soon he was laughing and standing on his head for the delighted children and the dog, who stood on his hind legs and nosed at the open window. It was a brief but happy interlude. Even Mrs. Riley smiled a little.

As we were about to move on, George told me that I was "not to worry none," they would follow right behind me all the way into Salt Lake City. If I should have any more trouble, they would be right there to fix me up.

Then he asked, "By the way, watcha got in that there Ford? That's the heaviest thing I ever took up a mountain."

When I told him it was full of books, he looked at me in total astonishment, and then half to himself murmured, "What on earth would a body ever do with that many *books*?"

His wife told me in a plaintive aside that she'd had three books at home she wanted to bring along, but her husband wouldn't let her.

Later that night, I pulled into a filling station in Salt Lake City, and my wonderful, raggedy guardian angels pulled in right behind me. I assured them my car was running fine and would give no more trouble. I thanked them profusely, then had to practically force them to take some money. Since I knew they had been sleeping out and eating meagerly, I've always hoped they had a good meal that night and found a comfortable place to stay with soft beds and a bath.

Smiling and waving, they drove away while Elmer trilled wistfully after them.

Early the next morning Elmer and I were on the road again. Although it was still about 650 miles to Walla Walla, I was sure I could make it by evening. The Ford was running fine. I didn't anticipate any more trouble.

Elmer, riding on my shoulder, enjoyed the sights of the city while the balmy morning air caressed our faces. It was a good time for traveling. I had just told Elmer we would drive across the city and stop on the other side for breakfast, when suddenly the car began to pull sideways to the sickening flop, flop of a flat tire.

We limped to the nearest garage where I asked to have the tire changed.

The brisk, white-coated attendant looked all the tires over carefully, then informed me that the other three were also in bad condition and strongly advised new ones all the way around. Since my knowledge of tires was based solely on whether they were flat or inflated, I wasn't in much condition to judge for myself. With all the trouble I'd had, I didn't want to take any more chances. Consequently, I left instructions that the car be serviced and equipped with a complete set of new tires. Elmer and I then hunted up a restaurant and had breakfast.

After that, we walked and waited and worried. At least I worried. Would I ever get to that meeting in Walla Walla? Most ministers and lay representatives would have arrived the night before, attended the evening inspirational meeting, had a good night's sleep, and arisen early for breakfast and the busy agenda of the day. Already the bishop would have gaveled to order the opening session of Conference.

I wondered if the superintendent of Eastern Washington, in whose district I had elected to serve, would hold a church for me. Or would he conclude that I was not coming and appoint someone else? I also wondered when the ordinations would take place and earnestly hoped they would be toward the end of the week so I'd have time to prepare myself. Another concern was that it had been several years since I had attended a Conference, and I needed time to find out what was going on in the area and what causes needed emphasis during the coming year.

Elmer, who always loved walks on city streets, enjoyed the one this morning more than usual. He was tired of much travel and few people. Occasionally he even loosened his hold around my neck and put forth a friendly hand to one of the broadly smiling people we met.

It was almost noon when we left the garage. Since we had been delayed yet again, I mentally set my arrival in Walla Walla at midnight instead of late afternoon. Surely nothing else could possibly go wrong with the car. It rolled smoothly out of Salt Lake City and up Highway 30. The hours went by with only a brief stop for a late lunch.

We were three quarters of the way through Idaho and just outside Glenns Ferry when suddenly my tranquilly speeding Ford began to balk again.

Like a stubborn mule that had obstinately decided to stop and sit down, come what might, the car ran slower and slower, then shuddered to a dead standstill. All my efforts to start it again resulted only in a few despairing gasps, then silence.

There was nothing to do but go for help.

The car was far enough off the road not to impede traffic, so with a sigh, I put Elmer on my shoulder and stepped out onto pavement that was hot under the afternoon sun.

"Hope we don't have to walk too far in this heat," I told him, though I was the one bothered by it.

Miraculously, a small garage and filling station sat just around the bend ahead. There was only one man on duty. But after he had listened to my problem, he simply walked out, leaving his business unattended, and went back with me to the car.

After assuring himself that the Ford was not going to start, he told me to get in and guide it while he pushed. He placed his broad shoulders and strong back against the rear of that heavy vehicle, yelled "Here we go!" and propelled it to the garage.

The car's problem, the man told me, was a low battery and a faulty generator. So he recharged the battery and fixed the generator. By the time the vehicle was in running order again, he had put in well over two hours of time. Yet when

I asked what I owed, he said, "Oh, about a dollar and a half," and refused to take more.

The car ran fine now, but by the time we reached Caldwell, Idaho that evening, I was tired. Elmer was tired. And so much time had been lost that it would again be impossible to arrive at our destination that night. Reluctantly, I resigned myself to missing another half day of Conference and took a motel room for the night.

Alas! The next day trouble arose from a new direction. Monkey trouble! Elmer had been the perfect little traveling companion until this particular morning. While I got ready for the road, I turned him loose to run and play, and he decided to keep right on running and playing. To heck with all this travel!

When I said, "Come on, Elmer," he grinned and climbed the curtains. Dealing with this monkey had definitely increased my grab speed, but I was no match for that miniature imp this morning. It was clear that he had determined to take time off for play, and if I insisted on trying to catch him, he might as well get some fun out of it.

By the time I climbed onto a chair to snatch him off the top of a window, he was under the bed. If I started to crawl under the bed, he was up next to the ceiling. Several times he even managed to swish by and slap my hand, and all the little devils of Satan laughed through his eyes.

Elmer was having a ball. But it was something less than a ball for me! Conference had already been in session for a day and an evening and was now rousing itself for another day, the day on which I had expected to be there easily by noon. Now here was this laughing little fiend, playing games and living it up, just as though there was nothing else of importance in the whole world.

Elmer knew very well what was meant by "No, no" and "Come here." In fact, he seemed to understand almost every word spoken. Just to say in his presence that I was going some place was enough to send him into a tizzy if it appeared he wouldn't get to go along. Now, however, my threats to go off and leave him were to no avail. In fact, the little rogue acted as if the whole human language had suddenly become extinct.

In my desperation I decided it was time this monk learned some discipline.

I got a broom from the kitchenette and took after him, with no intent to hit him, but to show I meant business, to scare him just enough to slow him down.

The result was not what I had counted on. As I brandished that big broom, Elmer's innocent glee turned to terror. He fled from me screaming. I still couldn't catch him. Worse, that tiny, trusting creature stared down at me through fear-glazed eyes as though I were some dread monster he'd never seen before.

That did things to me. I threw down the broom and collapsed into a chair, feeling like the lowest and meanest individual on earth. Why was it, I wondered, that Elmer was so frightened of a broom?

Then I remembered that episode in the men's room at La Guardia Airport. The boys had batted him down with a broom! He hadn't forgotten, poor little guy. The terror was with him still.

Outside, the sun shone and the trees flashed emerald green. Inside, our room was dark and gloomy. It had been like that all along, I suppose, but the monkey's gaiety had filled it with life and brightness. Now, Elmer cowered atop a window and the gaiety was gone.

Rousing myself to do what should have been done in the first place, I put that hated broom out of sight, brought Elmer's cage in from the car and put some food in it. Then I sat down and began to talk to him in soothing tones, telling him to come down and eat his breakfast.

It took time—a lot of time. The day's Conference sessions were in full swing without me and any idea of making it there by noon was completely out of question. But no matter what, my immediate responsibility was to that little fear-filled monkey atop the window.

While sitting there coaxing Elmer, a crazy scene took form in the back of my mind: The bishop, robed and majestic, looked down at me and demanded, "Why were you so late?" And I replied meekly, "I was trying to catch a monkey." A bit of hysterical laughter bubbled to the surface as I visualized the Bishop's reaction to that: "Well, what else could one expect from a woman preacher?"

I held my breath as I saw Elmer gradually begin to relax. He moved a little on his curtain rod perch and then began to climb slowly, slowly down the curtain. At length he came across the floor and crept into his cage. He still wasn't communicating with me, however.

He clambered onto his swing with a piece of bread in one hand, then began to swing and munch, swing and munch while the clock ticked away. Finally, he looked up at me and uttered a few soothing let's-make-up sounds.

I felt reprieved! I reached into the cage to caress him. He clung to a finger and leaned against my hand. We both felt better.

Soon we were in the car and on our way again. Elmer rode on my shoulder with his tail and arms tight around my neck. And he said kind things in my ear, while I reached often to pat and reassure him.

We arrived at Walla Walla some time that afternoon, almost two days late. But not bad, I thought, considering all the troubles and delays.

I managed to contact both the district superintendent and the bishop shortly before dinner. My district superintendent described the church to which he wished to appoint me and asked if this met with my approval.

I said, "Yes," and thanked him.

Actually, I knew nothing about any parishes in Eastern Washington. I had requested an appointment to the dryer side of the state for health reasons.

The bishop said my credentials were in order and that the ordinations would not be until Saturday. He was kind, not the type of man I had visualized that morning while coaxing Elmer down from his perch.

Later, after the evening meeting, I stood in the June night and held Elmer. I looked up at the stars and gratitude flowed through my whole being. Gratitude for being saved from a serious wreck, for all those kind individuals who had helped me along the way, and for this little monkey who had spread cheer and acted as a link of friendship between me and the people we met.

I did not realize then that in time I would forget every bit of the oratory and business of the Conference, but I would vividly remember my small traveling companion and all the Good Samaritans on our two thousand miles of Jericho Road.

≫ 9 ≪

The Parish

It was next to the last day of Conference and I felt good. School was behind me and I was fairly on tiptoe with eagerness to get on with my work. After more than three years of cramped living in small rooms and apartments, I could hardly wait to collect my books and furniture and live in a real house again.

This upsurge of desire for a house surprised me, since I had long felt that my former love of homemaking had been buried with my husband, Ray. Now I was grateful for the stirring of an old instinct, though still keenly conscious of the fact that home could never be the same without my husband. I thought wistfully of my sons, but knew they were living their own lives and would no longer be with me except for visits.

"At least I have Elmer," I consoled myself. "He'll liven things up for me!"

Well, it could be that he would liven things up too much. After all, my new home would be the church parsonage at

Mabton, a place I had never even heard of until a few days before. Perhaps the people there wouldn't take kindly to a monkey in the parsonage. For that matter, perhaps they wouldn't take kindly to a woman in the pulpit!

I was too full of anticipation, however, to harbor such thoughts for long. This was what I had dreamed of and worked toward—to serve again as the full-time pastor of a parish.

With gratitude I remembered the people on the Blanchard Circuit, to whom I had once ministered. Members of that circuit of five churches had given their support and whole-hearted acceptance to this "woman minister." And, being such warmly humane individuals, they would have loved Elmer. I was sure there would be equally kind people in other churches. God was good, life was good. Everything was going to be just fine!

Then one of my colleagues called me aside.

From his lofty height the clergyman peered down at me out of severe eyes set in a long, vertically lined face.

"Young lady, I want to talk to you. I understand you are being sent to the church in Mabton." Without waiting for my reply, he continued in his rumbling, man-of-the-cloth voice. "Now I want to tell you something. I know about those people where you are going, and I want to warn you here and now: keep that—that monkey of yours out of sight! And don't ever, ever be seen walking down the streets of Mabton with that thing on your shoulder!"

He nearly choked at the mere idea, but managed to continue pontifically, "Remember, you're going there to serve the Lord, not to be an ambulating circus."

That anyone should feel it necessary to remind me of my calling wounded me. Yet, as I looked into this man's humorless eyes, I wondered if a monkey wouldn't have helped him serve the Lord better. At least, my little monkey would have broadcast happiness wherever he went, and that seemed to me an important element of Christianity.

I promised the minister meekly enough, though vaguely, that I would be careful, then took off as gracefully as I could.

But he hurled a parting volley at my back. "Remember now, keep that animal out of sight! You're going to have enough trouble as it is!"

That last remark, of course, was in reference to the "unfortunate" fact that I was a woman. But I remembered anew my previous experience in the ministry when gender had not been a hindrance. At least, not after the shock of the first encounter.

However, that was before I became mother to a monkey. The warning that I must keep Elmer out of sight troubled me. Could it be possible that I was going to be thrown into an entire community of people as rigid and narrow as the person who had just chastised me?

My naturally optimistic self refused to believe it. And yet—and yet! This man certainly had more experience than I. He said he knew about the people where I was going. Could he be right?

As soon as Conference ended, Elmer and I set off across the state to get the stored furniture from my former home. On the way, I detoured to get a glimpse of Mabton.

The church was not far from the highway and easy to find. There it stood among the trees, chaste and white on a green grass lawn, its steeple reaching heavenward. I imagined the bell being rung on Sunday morning and wondered what kind of people went up and down the front steps of this lovely place.

The parsonage, only three blocks away, was a small, white house with a lawn that stretched out roomily at the back. A nice place for Elmer to play, I thought, if I dared let him be seen.

On my way back to the highway, I toured the treeless business area that lay languid and silent under a hot noonday sun. There was a graceful old bank building and a restaurant with a nice appearance. But other buildings had loose boards and peeling paint. There were several taverns in varying states of disrepair. A ragged man lolled in the doorway of one of these, while a few paces down the street a spotted dog, lying in a chipped-out hollow of broken sidewalk, lifted his head lazily. The monkey whistled at them, but they didn't seem to notice. I said, "Elmer, do you suppose that man and that dog will object to us living in their town?"

We reached the coast and were immediately involved in joyous reunions with friends, and especially with my son Paul and his wife. Paul was now out of the Service and back running the family farm.

But most of my time was taken up with business matters and getting furniture and goods packed for the movers. Through it all the clergyman's warning about being seen with a monkey in Mabton nagged at the back of my mind.

On the day the moving van left for my new home, I stayed behind for about three hours to take care of last minute details. It was Saturday afternoon and I had to drive those long miles back over the Cascade Mountains and beyond. And somehow I had to get a little sleep that night in order to face the members of a new congregation and conduct a church service the next morning.

By the time I reached Mabton it was around midnight. In spite of deep weariness, I thrilled to the soft, balmy air and to the stars sharp and bright in the night sky. I passed the shadowy white church and drove on to the parsonage.

Elmer had slept all across the spectacular mountains, through stands of forest, and acres of farm land. He always did. He didn't care two cents about the landscape, but he loved bright lights and people and never failed to wake up the moment we hit a town or city.

Tonight was no exception. By now he was jumping up and down in his cage and ready for excitement. I just hoped there would be something to drop down on for a bit of sleep.

The moving van would have been unloaded and gone long ago. It never occurred to me there would be anyone around at this time of night to meet me.

But there was. The house lights were all on. And as I pulled into the garage, two tall men stepped forward. I crawled out of the car, all rumpled and groggy, and did my best to be bright and brisk as I shook hands with them. They seemed friendly and kind. Nonetheless, I sensed their mingled surprise and amusement as they looked down at me. I'd heard it spoken so often that I knew what they were thinking. "She doesn't *look* like a preacher."

But who could blame them?

A smallish, five-foot-three woman in blouse, skirt, and ankle socks, with tousled hair and sleepy eyes didn't look like much of anything, let alone a minister. People expected their minister to be a man, or at the very least, someone with mannish looks and hair in a tight bun.

I wished wildly that Elmer would shut up and keep still. He was in semi-darkness on his side of the seat. But he rattled his cage like mad and whistled and chattered for attention.

I made a hasty exit through the garage door, hoping the men would follow me to the house and we could just ignore him. Perhaps they'd think he was a bird. At that moment I simply wasn't up to confessing to these two that their new minister had a skeleton—a monkey—in her closet.

However, the men did not follow my lead. They said, "Here, here, let us carry your things in," and began to open the car doors.

Well, there he was, that tiny morsel of a monk. And he was grinning at the men, reaching for them with his hands, and now and again doing fast loop-the-loops on his swing.

The warning of my dour advisor thundered through my mind—"Keep that monkey out of sight!" but what came out of my mouth was a jaunty "Gentlemen, meet Elmer!"

Well, the stars didn't fall from the sky. Neither was there any reaction to speak of from the men. One of them muttered softly, "I'll be darned!" Then they carried my luggage into the house, fixed a place for me to sleep, and went away.

I was too tired to wonder what they thought, or how I would handle my "sinful" situation with the other members of the parish. I fell asleep as my head hit the pillow.

The clock alarmed all too soon the next morning. After finding something for myself and Elmer to eat, I tethered him with a long sturdy ribbon to a heavy iron skillet in the middle of the floor. Here he could exercise, play and explore among the boxes. And I could put him in his cage when the time came to leave without first having to get him down from the top of a window or light fixture.

While Elmer played and chattered, I dressed, then sat down to compose myself, meditate, and get mentally prepared for the day's activities: Sunday School at ten, the church service at eleven, and a potluck dinner on the church lawn afterward.

Would they really welcome me? Was there a remote possibility that these people could be like the clergyman said? I looked at my happy little monkey, so small and innocent and voluble. How could I ever keep him a secret, even if I wanted to?

Sunday School was under way by the time I got to the church and an adult class was meeting in the sanctuary. I knew I didn't make a very commanding impression, but after all, I *was* the new minister. Therefore I had assumed that someone would at least stand up to greet me when I entered.

Not a soul paid me the slightest bit of attention.

I sat down unobtrusively while the teaching and discussion continued. Presently a rather large woman sitting in front of me turned and waved an imperious hand. "There's a draft in here. Go shut that door."

I went and closed the door.

After a time the class ended, the people stood up and moved about and visited, but still, no one even glanced my way. Finally, when I heard one person say to another, "Why in the world isn't the new minister here?" I stepped forward and said, "I'm the new minister."

The room went dead still.

After an awkward moment the woman who had ordered me to close the door said incredulously, "You? Why, you don't look like a minister!" Then she added, "I'm sorry. When I told you to shut the door, I thought you were one of the high school girls."

I chuckled to myself, half flattered.

Then, for no apparent reason, I suddenly felt free and happy, and a little reckless. So I was a woman! So I didn't look like a man! So I did have a monkey! If I were going to perform any real service in this parish, I would have to first be myself, and the people would either accept me as I was, including that little ol' monkey, or not at all.

Consequently, when I came to the part in the church service where new ministers usually tell their congregations something about themselves and their families, I told them about myself, about my parents, about my three sons, where they were and what they were doing.

Then I added, "The only member of my family with me at this time is up at the parsonage. He's a baby monkey, and his name is Elmer."

There! It was out. And I felt good, though perhaps a bit defiant. A flicker of movement passed through the congregation, but my usual sensitivity to people's reactions must not have been working very well that morning, for I really couldn't tell how they reacted.

Anyway, I forgot all about it for the time being and concentrated on the worship service. The sermon, as I remember, was something about the love of God and human friendship. I wanted to be friends with these people for it seemed to me that a solid basis of friendship between pastor and congregation is mandatory to any real accomplishments by a church.

The picnic and visiting after the service were pleasant if a bit restrained. I went home still unsure about how they would accept *me*, let alone the monkey.

However, in the following days, things began to happen. Callers came to the parsonage. Lots and lots of callers. Some came to talk about their problems. Some came to discuss particular areas of work in the church. But most came, I'm certain, purely out of an urge to be kind and friendly. And to see the monkey.

Elmer cooperated in an all-out effort to win them over. He whistled and chattered happily as the callers came up the walk. Once they were inside, if he was in his cage, he'd grin widely and reach out a tiny hand. This got the desired results. Most people, it seemed, were only too happy to shake hands with a monkey.

A handshake was merely the beginning as far as Elmer was concerned. He aimed to please and had his own ways of doing it. Once he had gained the complete attention of his guests, he often pretended to be utterly oblivious of their presence. He performed all sorts of feats, at times with his back to them. Periodically, though, he cast a quick, sly look over his shoulder to see how they were taking it. He stood on his head, did somersaults, and most everything children do on the playground, plus a lot more tricks of his own invention.

One of his star cage acts was to get on his swing, kick it into earth-shaking momentum, then in full flight whip himself around his seat bar in such a manner as to form a loop when he grabbed the tip of his tail in his mouth. After this, one saw only a dizzying circle of furry black careening madly back and forth.

Often, visitors found him down on the floor diapered and tethered by his long ribbon to the iron skillet. At such times the entertainment was entirely different.

If the caller happened to be a woman and reasonably well-behaved, Elmer would not only honor her by holding her fingers, but he would even sit on her lap, look her straight in the eye and carry on some serious monkey conversation. Then, with the preliminaries over, he'd get down to what he'd planned to do all along: investigate her clothes. He became utterly absorbed as he scrutinized every pocket, every bead, every ruffle, every tiny button; he became so absorbed in fact, that he sometimes forgot to note whether anyone was watching. When he was all through with the top layer of her clothing, Elmer wasn't above flipping up the lady's skirt to find out what exciting, lacy things might be underneath.

Women were usually Elmer's favorite people but there were some men he found exceedingly interesting, especially if they were hairy. When he met a man, the first thing he did was run a small hand expertly up under the man's pant leg. If hair was plentiful, oh, what a find! However, when he made the discovery that hair grew on men's chests, he was in seventh heaven!

One day one of the most dignified men in town stopped by, along with his equally formal wife. When Elmer began to feel around under the man's trouser leg, I thought it high time to remove him to other parts of the house. But as I scooped up the protesting monkey and started out of the room, the man said, "Uh... why don't you just let him stay?"

So Elmer stayed, and was in ecstasy. After he had examined all that leg hair, he proceeded to climb the man's ample frame and took time to examine every detail along the way. The pockets were given special thought, and all their contents taken out, duly noted, and put back. Then he went up over the paunch and paused briefly to ponder that bright zipper. I had a moment of pure agony there, because I knew how fast those nimble hands could open a zipper. Fortunately, this one didn't interest him today. Zippers were old stuff. He'd been given lots of them to play with.

He proceeded to the chest. In a flash, Elmer had our guest's top collar button undone. Then the next one down and the one below that.

And what a discovery! A vast expanse of black, curly hair! Here was something worthy of real scientific investigation. Elmer set to work in earnest, carefully parting first one section and then another. Then he popped something—a flake of salt, I suppose—into his mouth.

I held my breath. Elmer was taking far too many liberties. When he again popped something into his mouth, the man's wife burst into laughter. "Looks like you've got fleas, Henry!" she said.

Henry responded with a deep belly laugh that shook him and the monkey all over. But Elmer clung to that hair and kept right on with his work. When the man could finally speak, he looked down at Elmer and said, "Why, you little devil! You darned little devil!"

I can't say how it happened, but before these two took their leave, we were all sitting on the floor playing with the monkey.

This was a pattern that would be repeated over and over. The most decorous and proper people who came to call often ended up sitting on the floor, laughing like children while they played with Elmer.

Sometimes, people came with really important matters to discuss. Then I had the problem of either forcibly removing Elmer from the living room or almost forcing my callers to the study.

But if the adults came to see the minister and stayed to play with the monkey, the children frankly came to see the monkey and sometimes lingered to visit me. Most of the youngsters came first with their parents. Then they came back without their parents. Then they came back bringing their friends. Then their friends brought friends.

A little boy named Joe came all by himself one day. He said, without preamble, "I want to join your church."

I replied, "I thought you went with your parents to the church across town. Why do you want to be a member here?"

My young caller replied with scorn, "Our pastor doesn't even have a *cat!* "

I persuaded him that he should continue to go to church with his parents, but that he could still come often to see Elmer and me.

Joe and the other children usually came bearing gifts. I once made a list of Elmer's most recent gift collection. It included: string, balls, peanuts, pictures, tin cans, rubber bands, oranges, bananas, an egg beater, pencils, notebooks, chewing gum, belts, zippers, bandaids, toy guns, buttons, and all-day suckers. Elmer loved it all, both the attention and the gifts.

Those gifts afforded him endless amusement. He could work an egg beater, chew gum, scribble on paper, admire bright pictures, and put on bandaids with the best of them.

The children were especially delighted to see the monkey take his bottle, and he was equally delighted to show them how he did it. Teetering back on his heels and curled up tail, he would hoist that doll bottle of milk and swig it down with verve. He could give the act variations too. When he was in an extra happy mood, he sometimes took his bottle standing on his head, tail anchored to his swing.

While watching Elmer, the children often told me about their kittens and puppies and baby brothers and baby sisters. Animal or human, they were all in the same class as far as these youngsters were concerned. Oddly enough, the mothers, while discussing this small monkey, talked to me about *their* children's cute tricks, illnesses, and behavior.

The monkey was kept in his cage while I was away or working extra hard at home, but he was such a sociable little person that his cage had to be moved to the study or whatever room I happened to occupy. There he crooned to me contentedly about how nice it was to have just the two of us home together. When I became too absorbed in typing or reading to pay any further attention to his chatter, he took a nap or played with his toys or scribbled with his pencil.

There were limits to his patience, however. If I was oblivious to the world for too long a time, he might resort to drastic measures to bring me out of it—like throwing spitwads at me or just screeching. And before I obtained a padlock, he would simply break out of the cage and go mad-capping about the place—up and onto the tops of doors, up curtains and across the tops of windows, up and down lamps, while every now and then hurling himself at my desk to swipe a pen, a letter, a handful of sermon notes, or whatever he thought I considered most valuable. That was always a sure-fire way to get my attention.

There was no ordinary cage door fastener—a hook, a tightly tied cord, or a twisted wire—that Elmer couldn't undo in short order if he set his mind to it.

Once I got a padlock, however, all this escape artist business stopped, though he could and would have unlocked the padlock if the key had ever been left where he could reach it.

But one couldn't keep a monkey, even this very small one, shut up in a cage all the time. Whenever we were alone and I could spare time to keep an eye on him, Elmer was let out of the cage to run and climb to his heart's delight. In the kitchen he loved to run like mad to get up momentum, then collapse his small body and slide on the waxed floor. He also enjoyed having me lie down on the floor and prop my feet up on a chair, so he could slide down my bare legs. But he liked most of all to climb and explore. More than once, before I could get across the room to grab him, Elmer ran up a cupboard door, opened it, located a certain bowl, plunged a greased-lighting hand into it, and tore off with a fistful of sugar.

Through all this, I prepared sermons, conducted worship services, sent out newsletters, called on the people of the parish, conducted weddings and funerals, and went to

meetings—youth groups, women's meetings, men's meetings, and commission and church board meetings. So the days sped by.

Now, whenever I remembered my colleague's dire warning to "keep that monkey out of sight," I didn't feel at all disturbed, and whenever I went down the street with Elmer on my shoulder, all the people smiled.

Elmer and I smiled back.

⇒ 10 ⇐

Capuchin Cupid

After a short time in the Mabton pastorate, I attended the annual Pastor's School at the University of Puget Sound in Tacoma. This week-long refresher course meant a four-hour drive to the coast, and then an extra hundred miles north to leave Elmer in the care of my son Paul and his wife.

The Pastor's School proved to be a refresher course in more ways than I expected. Once rid of Elmer, I had planned to give my entire attention to the three eminent scholars who had come to instruct and inspire us. But there was a fourth clergyman there who upstaged the others for me.

As I walked toward the registration desk, there he was —tall, substantially built, handsome, and with a certain dignified courtliness. However, that dignity was held in check ever so slightly by a perky black mustache. He nodded, and the blue eyes above the black mustache twinkled as they swept over me. It was a look that left me both flattered and flustered. I quickly turned and began filling out enrollment papers at the desk.

I'm sure I don't know how it all came about, but I found this man sitting beside me at lunch, at dinner, and at both the afternoon and evening lecture sessions. Then, by ten o'clock that evening, when our more sensible colleagues were going to bed, we were going out on a date.

We had already discovered a good deal about each other. Among other things, he knew that I was Gertrude Dealy, a widow, that I had gone back to school after the death of my husband, and that I had just graduated and become paster of the Mabton church in Eastern Washington. And I knew that he was Palmer Sorlien, a widower serving a church in Portland.

We talked for hours that night. I discovered that he had what was for me the priceless ability to laugh at oneself. I also discovered that he did not hesitate to go after what he wanted. At least, not on this occasion.

He asked me to marry him!

He was rash, he was insane, he was wonderful! But naturally I said, "No." A person this impetuous was not to be trusted, I told myself.

Also, a man who proposes to a woman on their first date is surely asking for more than he knows. Palmer didn't know that if he got me, he'd get a monkey thrown in for good measure.

Our week at Tacoma was nearly over before I got around to telling him about Elmer. When I did, the reaction was surprising. Palmer stepped back a pace, arched his dark brows, and asked suspiciously, "Where does this monkey sleep?"

I lifted my chin and replied firmly, "With me, of course!"

This man had been escorting me about for a week, all the while murmuring promises of every delightful thing in Heaven and on earth if only I would consent to be his wife. But now he said, as though giving a decree from Mount Sinai, "I will not sleep with a monkey!"

My reply was to the point. "Nobody asked you to!"

I whirled away and left him standing on the campus green.

Palmer tracked me down a little later, chuckled over the whole episode, and was as gallant as ever. But he still maintained, though with a touch of humor, that he would not sleep with a monkey. And I still reminded him that I had by no means promised to marry him, let alone give up my small bedfellow.

Even aside from the monkey and the suddenness of Palmer's proposal, all the circumstances of my life at this time were against marriage. Not the least of these were the intense ties that still bound me to my husband, Ray Dealy, who had died four years before. My children had told me that they would not be adverse to my remarriage. But at this point I was emotionally unprepared to accept the fact that I need not love my former husband any less in order to love another. Even had my feelings been otherwise, I would have refused the man's proposal. I scarcely knew him!

However, we did seem to get along well. If only he would forget about this marriage business, we ought to be able to enjoy good times together at occasional meetings in the future.

In the future?

Back home after the Pastor's School, I was trying feverishly to get caught up with parish work, and had been home only three days when Palmer phoned to say, "I'm coming up to see you tomorrow."

I wondered why in the world I had gotten myself romantically involved while still new in this parish and with such a heavy schedule of work. He wasn't someone I could ever be serious about. So instead of those feeble remonstrations, why had I not said a flat "No!" when he phoned to say he was coming?

That morning, I raced into the house from a round of calls and took Elmer out of his cage for some brief cuddling. It would be an unheard of thing for my small Capuchin not to get his hugging and loving session after being left alone. While the monkey rode on my shoulder with his arms around my neck, I quickly fixed his lunch: a tiny piece of toast, a sliver of vegetable, and his doll bottle of milk.

Back in the cage, Elmer swigged down his milk then sat in his swing and leisurely ate his meal, all the while chattering to me above the roar of the vacuum cleaner.

I was cleaning up spitwads. They littered the floor in a wide circumference around his cage. When alone, Elmer's favorite way of passing the time was to throw spitwads. Tearing a sliver from the paper which lined the bottom of his cage, he chewed a bit of it until wet, rolled it industriously between his hands, then with speed and accuracy, hurled it through the air to an astonishing distance. Astonishing, that is, considering the size of the thrower.

As I chased the vacuum cleaner back and forth, I reflected on how much less work I'd have to do without that monkey. Much less floor cleaning, no cage to wash, no monkey to diaper, feed and fuss over. Not that I had any notion of getting rid of this source of my woes.

You couldn't just say to a baby monkey who covered you with kisses and looked at you with big, adoring eyes—you couldn't just say, "You're too much trouble," and then cast him out. No, not that. Not even if he did threaten to come between you and someone you rather liked.

As I sped through a flurry of arranging books and papers in my study, dusting the house, and bringing in flowers, I wondered how Elmer would take to my special guest. He liked most people, but when he chose to dislike someone, he seemed to have his reasons. In such an instance he would trust neither himself nor me with the object of his dislike.

I recalled an incident that occurred while I was still in school at SMU. A would-be suitor came to call one Sunday afternoon. At first the man went to Elmer's cage and tried to strike up an acquaintance, but the monkey would have none of him. He just turned his back in cold disapproval. When the man sat down beside me, Elmer began to scold in no uncertain terms. In spite of this unfriendly barrage, the two of us managed to visit until the guest reached to take hold of my hand.

Then all hell broke loose.

Elmer let out the most awful screams I'd ever heard —long, sustained, blood-curdling. Suddenly Mrs. Swenson was pounding on the back door to my room while the occupants of the adjoining apartment were beating on the wall between us. And all of them were yelling, "What's the matter in there? What's wrong?"

I yelled some inane explanation while letting my uncomfortable visitor out the front door. He never came back.

Now, I wondered about that man. I was sure he hadn't had murder in mind as the monkey seemed to think. But could there have been something about him that was not quite on the up and up?

Well, that meeting had been relatively unimportant, but this one would be a little different. I certainly didn't intend to marry Palmer, but I liked him and I wanted Elmer also to think well of him. I had enough on my mind right then without having to try to figure out who was right, Elmer or I, in case of a difference of opinion. And I wanted this caller to be able to at least touch me without that monkey calling in all the neighbors.

Still another possible complication was the fact that my elegant suitor appeared to have made up his mind in advance that he wasn't going to like Elmer. Heaven help us if the feeling between them should be mutual.

Soon the house was in order. Elmer, neat and tidy in his cage, was curled up on his blanket, sleepy-eyed and drowsily sucking his thumb. I paused in the doorway to look out upon the lush summer day: all blue sky, green grass and warm sun. I had only to powder my nose and brush my hair but there was still plenty of time, I told myself. Palmer had said he would arrive at about two o'clock. It was now only 1:15.

At that moment a long, shiny automobile glided up the street and came to a stop in a cloud of dust at my gate. "How unfortunate," I thought, "to have a visit from a parishioner just now."

Then out stepped the Reverend John Palmer Sorlien. All spruce and happy and expectant.

There was a moment of panic when I almost turned to run for a mirror and comb, but instead headed for the gate. I hated to admit to myself how good it was to see this guy again! We shook hands decorously and stood there for a moment looking at each other. Then Palmer bowed and with a flourish gestured toward the new car.

"Bought it just for you!" he said. Meaning, of course, that it was for me when I became his wife. The nerve of this man! But I was charmed in spite of myself.

Well, he hadn't met Elmer yet. Perhaps he'd take back the offer of his fine car then.

We strolled up the walk. I was slightly tousled as usual and Palmer was correct in every detail as usual: dark suit, white shirt, proper tie, shined shoes.

When we entered the living room, Elmer was sitting up awaiting us. Now alert and wide-eyed, he still had his thumb in his mouth, but the eyes above the thumb scrutinized the stranger. After a short time he removed his thumb long enough to monkey-talk about the time of day, then popped it back into his mouth and sucked leisurely, while he continued to solemnly observe all that went on.

When Palmer and I sat down side by side, Elmer objected mildly, then when Palmer actually touched my hand, he objected more vigorously. But suddenly this negative attitude was reversed. The monk went into a wild, cage shaking demonstration of attention-getters and good will: swinging by two arms, swinging by one arm, swinging by his tail, turning somersaults and standing on his head.

Elmer, it seems, had accepted our guest. But had our guest accepted Elmer? I saw no signs that this man, who seemed to be so enamored of me, a mere woman, was at all swept off his feet by this scintillating, captivating monkey.

Palmer put up at a hotel in Sunnyside and stayed around for three days, with no change in his detached attitude toward Elmer. Then he went back to Portland. After all, we both had responsibilities.

During the summer he came back again and again, and again. I don't know how he managed to be away from work so much, but his parishioners never seemed to complain. As a matter of fact, when I later visited his church, I gathered that his people were devoted to him and would have been reluctant to criticize him for anything.

As for the people of my parish, they were delighted with this urbane gentleman, who soon became a friend of almost everyone in town. There were sly little smiles wherever we showed up together, though I never sensed anything but approval in their attitude.

"Reverend Sorlien is a fine man," they told me, "a fine man." It was almost as though they were trying to help me make up my mind about him. Even Elmer did everything he could to further the romance. He trilled and whistled with joy, grinned and held out his hands each time Palmer came.

Elmer was not allowed his usual run of the house when Palmer came to visit. Then, his play area outside the cage was confined to a radius of about six feet—the length of the cloth leash that tied him to the iron skillet. At such times it was difficult for Palmer to walk across the room without Elmer grabbing him. Palmer always disengaged himself quickly and that was that.

This aloofness, however, in no way dampened Elmer's ardor. He continued to look at our guest with shiny-eyed admiration. He talked to him, he wrote for him, he did all his gymnastic stunts. He drank from his bottle standing on his head. But all he ever got from that man was an occasional reluctant grin.

I was silently indignant. Well, this guy didn't have to like my monkey if he didn't want to. Why should I care? I hadn't promised to marry him and probably wouldn't!

One hot evening after Palmer had taken me out to dinner, I found that I had to make an emergency call at the home of a parishioner. Palmer, who was expecting to spend more time with me before going back to his hotel, said he would wait until I returned. Elmer had been caged too long and insisted on being let out. I quickly removed him from the cage, attached his leash to the skillet and gave him his doll and various playthings. The davenport was within climbing distance but Palmer could take the easy chair at the far end of the room and read in peace while I was gone.

The call took much longer than I had expected. On my return I came in quickly but quietly by the back way, hoping to surprise them by my sudden appearance. But it was I who got the surprise! I stood transfixed in the door to the living room, while the scene before me engraved itself upon my memory.

Palmer was sitting on the davenport in his shirt sleeves with small black Elmer ensconced cozily on his white shirted shoulder. There was a bemused expression in the man's eyes and a funny little smile on his lips. Elmer had helped himself to the black date book from Palmer's shirt pocket, and he turned the pages slowly, studying each one with the utmost concentration. Now and again he looked up into Palmer's eyes to make an earnest comment, seemingly about something he had just read; or he nestled his tiny, dusky face against Palmer's cheek, and made those small comforting sounds he used when utterly content.

Palmer's newspaper lay unopened across his knees, and every little while he reached up to stroke the monkey caressingly. He had capitulated at last!

I coughed. Palmer jumped and looked guilty, but he didn't push the monkey away. I went in and sat down beside them, whereupon Elmer went into a state of pure rapture as he tried to make us understand how right and good it was for the three of us to be sitting there together.

It did seem right and good. Yet when Palmer left that night, after asking me again for about the thousandth time to marry him, I still could not say yes.

Nevertheless, after that night I began to instigate some changes in our sleeping arrangements. From early babyhood the monkey had slept with his tail and body curled tightly around my neck. In those first days of our life together, Elmer had been such a forlorn and lost little thing that when I tried to go to bed without him, all that heart-rending baby crying simply demolished me. So I got up and took him from his cage to my bed. There he anchored himself around my neck, popped a thumb into his mouth, sucked and grunted contentedly, and soon fell fast asleep.

In his baby days, when there seemed to be no weight to him at all, I didn't mind. Not until summer came, anyway. Then those hot Texas nights got a bit uncomfortable with that small furpiece around my neck. Now, however, he was more than a year and a half old and had a little weight to him, and it was summer in Eastern Washington, another hot climate. I became even more uncomfortable sleeping with Elmer curled tight around my neck. If I turned in my sleep, he adjusted himself accordingly but he never let go.

Though Palmer and Elmer were now good friends, that still didn't mean that Palmer would take kindly to sleeping with a monkey. Of course, this had no bearing on the case at all, I told myself. I was going to make the change simply for my own comfort.

My determination to make a change in our manner of sleeping was one thing. Getting Elmer to agree to it was quite another. As long as I sat up and studied, the monkey could sleep peacefully in his cage beside me, even to three or four o'clock in the morning. But when I went to bed, he fully expected to go with me. The mere idea of sleeping in the dark by himself was incomprehensible.

At first his cage was placed in the bathroom which opened off my bedroom. I arranged the monkey comfortably inside on his pad, put a light cover over him, then patted him gently and said, "Go to sleep, Elmer. Go to sleep."

He looked at me as though I couldn't possibly realize what I was saying. He knew very well what "go to sleep" meant, but he was certain this was no proper place to bed down for the night.

When I turned out the light and went to bed, Elmer promptly but politely reminded me that I had forgotten him. When he either got no answer or just a "Go to sleep," he became exasperated and began to scold at the top of his voice. I thought surely he would stop after a time, but he didn't. Rather, the scolding turned into a long, terrified crescendo of screaming. The windows were open to the hot night and I worried that he would disturb our neighbors just across the fence.

But I broke before they did. I sprang out of bed, turned on the lights, and took this frightened little creature out of his cage to cuddle and reassure him. Then we went to bed to finish the night together. Elmer clamped himself tight around my neck, put his thumb in his mouth, and gradually gave way to sleep.

There was no immediate sleep for me. This was a problem that had to be solved without breaking Elmer's heart and mine as well. At long last, I hit upon a different procedure.

The next night I placed the monkey cage right beside me on my bed, put Elmer in it and told him to go to sleep. Again there was screaming and crying, but now he could reach out and touch me. He finally went to sleep, clinging tightly to one of my fingers. After he had finally grown accustomed to this, I gradually began to push his cage farther and farther away from me. There were more objections when he could no longer hold my finger, but these ceased at length, and he comforted himself with his thumb and the fact that when he called to me out of the dark, I would answer with reassurance, and sometimes a few small pats.

Finally the monkey and his cage could be moved to a table beside my bed, then eventually to the far side of the room. But it was to be a long while before he would tolerate being left in a dark room by himself.

Elmer continued to rejoice when Palmer came to see us. And it was to see *us* as far as he was concerned. Whenever Palmer and I sat down side by side, Elmer was right there to share in the togetherness. Palmer no longer seemed to mind. In fact, he appeared to enjoy it when the monkey climbed up to groom his hair, examine his eyebrows, his ears, and even, given half a chance, his teeth.

Palmer became so accustomed to this small pest that he could sit and talk to me for long stretches of time and act as though it were the most ordinary thing in the world that a monkey should all the while be examining his necktie, fingering his shirt buttons, or systematically emptying his pockets.

One day Palmer drove up from Portland and entered the house with a look of smug resolve on his face. Elmer was right there to take it all in when our guest, still standing in the middle of the floor, said to me, "Let me see your hands."

Unsuspecting, I put out my hands. He caressed my fingers one by one, then suddenly slipped a diamond onto my ring finger.

"There now," he said. "How soon can we set the date?"

I collapsed onto the davenport and stared stupidly at the ring. Elmer hopped up to my lap and he stared also. He bent over this sparkling thing with great curiosity and explored the diamonds with tiny, agile fingers. Palmer sat down beside me and urged, "Do you like it? Do you like it?"

I finally answered, "Yes. It's perfectly beautiful! But why did you do it? I haven't said I would marry you!"

He replied with an air of assurance, "Oh, you've just been taking too much time to make up your mind. And you're going to marry me anyway, so why not wear this ring?"

Well, why not indeed? After all, I had to admit I really loved this crazy, marvelous man—this man who knew what he wanted, and wouldn't take "no" for an answer.

And so it happened that on a certain autumn day a few weeks later, we went back to the University of Puget Sound where we had first met. There we stood together in the chapel and were married by the University President. After the service we went hand in hand back to the car where Elmer awaited us.

Palmer never slept with a monkey. But he did take one along on his honeymoon.

≫11≪

Christmas Train

Christmas fell on Sunday that year. The church people and I had shared an Advent season filled with carols, programs, and expectations of this day. Like Christmas observances around the world, our own worship service was a moving celebration of the birth of the Christ Child. Candles, poinsettias, manger scene, and softly luminous faces of men, women and children blended into one with the Scripture, the music, and the spoken word.

When the last song had been sung and benediction spoken, I did not linger at the door for the usual leave-taking ritual. The congregation approved of this omission, for they knew I had to catch the train at 12:30 for Seattle. The majority had their families with them for this important day, but I still had to cross the mountains before I could be with mine.

Most of the congregation followed to see me off. They had a special reason for this. They not only wanted to help but to see what would happen to their minister when she tried to smuggle a monkey onto a no-pets-allowed passenger train.

The train was the only way to spend Christmas with my family. Driving a car was out of the question for, aside from the time involved, warnings were out that the pass over the mountains was closed by ice and snow.

My family was gathering at the home of Glen and his wife in Seattle. Paul and his wife were driving down the coast from the farm while my husband was coming up from Portland. The only one who would not be present was Ross, who was on another motorcycle trip—this time through Africa.

Palmer planned to bring me home in a day or two when the pass would be cleared. But right now I *had* to get aboard that train. And my kind friends were eager to help.

At home I hastily showed the men my waiting luggage, then took Elmer out of his cage to put his coat on over his red jacket. That coat was a doll's blue kimono from the dime store. While I unceremoniously shoved the monkey into it, he looked at all those people and whimpered because he didn't understand what was going on. I reassured him as I placed him on his bed inside the cage. The cage was covered by a blanket pinned securely over all, except for a flap that could be lifted back from the door.

When I had purchased my ticket earlier, the agent had informed me that no pets were allowed on passenger trains. The only exception was for a caged bird. Since Elmer would be in his parrot cage, my friends and I reasoned (or perhaps I should say rationalized) that it surely couldn't make any great difference to the railroad officials if there happened to be a small monkey instead of a parrot in the cage.

We were across the tracks from the depot when the train came whistling down the rails and rolled majestically to a halt. The great black engine, at the head of the passenger train and a long tail of baggage and mail cars, chugged, spat and vibrated fearsomely amidst the snow. Elmer jumped about in his dark cage and asked questions of me and had to be comforted.

I was the only passenger from Mabton that day. Nearly everyone else was home getting ready for Christmas dinner—except, of course, the crowd that surrounded me as I carried my covered cage and waded through the snow toward the passenger coach.

The step was out and the conductor waited. He slapped his hands together sharply against the cold and eyed the cage as I drew near. I hoped fervently that he would just take it for granted that I carried a bird and let me on the train.

Then this grizzled man in the trim suit and smart cap demanded loudly, "Whatcha got there?"

I could feel the tension tighten among the gently conniving parishioners behind me as I slowly turned the cage around and lifted the blanket flap.

Elmer, with his red jacket collar sticking up above his long coat, tipped back his small dark head and looked up into the stern face of the conductor. Then he puckered his mouth into a round "o" and whistled at him—a long, trilling, questioning whistle. Then, satisfied that this was an okay guy, he grinned and stuck out a tiny hand in greeting.

A look of stupefaction slid over the rugged features of the conductor. For what seemed like an eternity to me, he just stood and stared at the monkey. Then the weathered lines of his face began to work oddly, and suddenly laughter boomed out of him: bellowed and boomed with the deep chug and swish of the engine up ahead. He leaned over to shake the small hand of the monkey, then straightened up and waved magnanimously toward the door of the coach.

"Oh, get on!" he said. "It's Christmas!"

Someone took my luggage from the men, then the conductor himself held the monkey cage while he assisted me up the steps. From the door I looked back at my smiling friends, and my heart was light. Yes, it really was Christmas!

The train was sparsely occupied at 12:30 on this Christmas day. Most people, not having to do things like preach a sermon that morning, were already at their destinations. I was glad for the nearly empty coach for I needed rest. In spite of my deep enjoyment of the Christmas season, the pace had taken its toll of my strength. Now I could just lean back and relax, and be bright and rested for the festivities with my family that evening.

The seat I chose had no one sitting in front of or behind me. Leaving the cage covered except for a peephole, I hoped to discourage the attention of any curious passenger strolling up the aisle. Perhaps Elmer and I would even be able to sleep all the way to Seattle.

The train let out a long, shrill whistle, jerked, then gathered momentum. Behind his peephole Elmer's dark eyes flared questions at me.

"It's all right," I told him and reached inside the cage to hold him and shuck off his coat. He seemed to take my word for it that things were okay. And when he saw that I curled up in a resting position, he also settled down. Lying on his small bed, he tucked a thumb in his mouth and gave a few contented grunts, always his prelude to sleep.

However, before Elmer's eyelids had time to droop, or I to even begin to relax, three men tramped down the aisle and headed straight for us. Any chance for that anticipated rest disintegrated as the conductor seated himself across the aisle, while the two brakemen settled into the seat back of us.

Soon one of the brakemen tapped me on the shoulder to ask if I would mind uncovering the cage so they could see the monkey. What could I do? After all, one might say Elmer was traveling under false pretenses. The least I could do was be obliging. I therefore removed the safety pins and peeled the blanket off the cage.

That was all Elmer needed to change his mood from sleepiness to celebration. He promptly climbed the cage wires with the light of adventure in his eyes. The men and Elmer laughed at each other. As soon as the monkey had made his brief preliminary judgement of them, he clung happily to their exploring fingers. The interest was mutual, for while the men poked and patted him as best they could through the wires, Elmer took every opportunity to thoroughly examine a fingernail, or to shoot his hand through the bars to finger the hair on the back of a big hand.

It was the stern looking man across the aisle, however, who did most of the talking. He asked all sorts of questions about the monkey. Periodically he stood up, pushed back his conductor cap, and bent over me to get his share of the monkey's attention.

"You know," he said, "this little critter reminds me of a damncoon I had once. He had hands just like Elmer's here, only bigger of course. And was he ever a pest! Why, we couldn't keep him in any kind of cage or pen. He was a

regular escape artist. And steal! That thing stole money, my
wife's jewelry, my watch, my keys. You name it. If it was
valuable, he stole it. Lord a-mighty, that damncoon just
made life hell for us all the time!"

Never once did this conductor just say "coon." He always
prefaced it with "damn" and ran the two words together. I
was fascinated by the man's face as he talked about his awful
coon. His voice was rough, his words accusing, yet his eyes
beneath their bushy brows were strangely alight, and the hint
of a grin that pushed at the hard lines of his face was almost
tender.

All the way across the snow-covered plains and up
toward the white mountain peaks, the conductor told me
about his coon. Now and then he righted his cap smartly and
hurried away on some errand. Then he came back, played a
bit with Elmer and continued his story.

He said, "My wife could have killed that damncoon the
day she found him plunging his hands into the honey jar and
licking his fingers.

"But that was nothing compared to her reaction the time
she found him washing a live mouse in the toilet bowl!
Coons wash things before they eat 'em, you know. My wife
was always deathly afraid of mice anyway, and I thought
she was gonna shoot right up through the
wild-blue-yonder!"

The brakemen behind me continued to hang over the
back of my seat to watch Elmer, and the monkey obligingly
went through his whole repertoire of tricks to entertain them.

But it was the conductor who talked to me continually,
as he sat sideways in his seat with his feet in the aisle and
recalled anecdotes about his coon. He had to move his feet

now and then as a passenger trekked past us on the way to the washroom. The passenger got a glimpse of an animated, black-haired monkey in a red jacket. Then he grinned and reluctantly went on.

The train sped along, now well down the west side of the mountains. The shrouded evergreens, peeking at us through their snowy veils, became ever bolder as their coverings grew thinner. The conductor's story of his coon continued.

"Seems like as he grew older, that damncoon just got worse and worse. He tore up gardens, and even broke into the neighbors' houses when they were gone. Hell, he always knew when they were away, no matter what. Then he'd tear off a window screen or something, even open a door if it wasn't locked, and go right in and raid the kitchen." The man's eyes held a thinly concealed light of pride at this revelation of the coon's dastardly behavior.

"Well, you can just imagine what a ruckus all that breaking and entering raised in the neighborhood! That damncoon was just too smart for his own good. Or mine either. And so," he concluded in a hard voice, "I got rid of him!"

Again the man's facial expressions recanted his words. I wanted to know how he got rid of his coon, but the sorrow in his eyes kept me from asking.

As the train entered the outskirts of Seattle, the two brakemen shook hands with Elmer and me and wished us a merry Christmas, then disappeared into another section of the train. The conductor also disappeared but was back as the train hissed to a slow-down near the Seattle depot. He picked up Elmer's cage and a suitcase and guided me to the door.

As the train slid to a final stand-still, the conductor lifted the flap of the cage and shook the small hand that was promptly thrust at him. Then he shook hands with me as he said, "You know, I'm mighty glad you had this little bugger here on the train, even if it is against regulations. It sure brought back memories to me of that damncoon!"

From the door, I could see that my husband waited in a light fall of snowflakes. The conductor handed the baggage, Elmer and me over to him, then resumed his stern expression. Palmer and I embraced happily, and from his cage Elmer tugged at Palmer's pant leg. As we turned to go, the conductor waved at us, then called out gruffly, "Have a merry Christmas, Elmer!"

⇒12⇐

Heartbreak

After our marriage, Palmer and I finished the church year at our respective locations, then were appointed to a church where we could serve together. It was hard to say goodbye to the Mabton folk who had taken us to their hearts during the year Elmer and I had been with them.

Our beautiful new church at St. Helens, Oregon, was a few miles north of Portland, and a considerably larger parish than I had served in Eastern Washington. Consequently, the parsonage became an even busier place, especially after the children found out about the monkey. Eventually it became necessary for me to have an office upstairs at the church in order to have some undisturbed time for study. I stocked this room with a typewriter, some of my most-used books, and a heap of playthings for Elmer.

Elmer loved it there. He especially enjoyed sitting on the window sill to view the world below. His sharp eyes never missed a thing, and sometimes he chattered with such excitement that I had to go to the window to see what was going on.

The monkey also enjoyed his playthings, which were mostly different from those at the house. Among them was an old alarm clock. One day while he was playing with it, I sat down on the floor with him and had his complete attention as I demonstrated how to wind the alarm, how to pull out the button to make it ring, and then how to slap down on the button to stop the ringing. When I gave the clock back to Elmer, he promptly wrapped himself, tail and all, around it to hold it steady and repeated the whole process exactly.

I was proud of this bright little fellow! Though there would be times when I questioned my own wisdom of teaching him how to operate an alarm clock. On many occasions I was suddenly blasted out of a period of deep concentration by the clattering, full-throated ringing of that clock. Elmer would gravely observe his clock, listen, and when finally satisfied, expertly slap down the alarm button. Sometimes I had a strong suspicion that he was doing more than just alarming the clock; he was tired of my silence and this was a sure way to bring me out of it.

Palmer's daughter, Meridith, whose husband was in the service, came to live with us at intervals while we were in St. Helens. When she arrived, Elmer sized up this new occupant in our home and seemed to conclude that here was competition for him. It wasn't exactly that he disliked Meridith, but he flat-out refused to let her tell him what, or what not, to do. And he certainly tried, at every opportunity, to put her in her place. Once Meridith, Palmer and I were sitting together on the sofa sharing sections of the daily paper while Elmer played across the room. Then Meridith

told on him. "Mama, look at Elmer, he's getting into your
church bulletin material!"

Elmer dropped the forbidden papers, turned, sashayed
across the room, and slapped her sharply on the leg. Then
he took off with the air of a little smarty-pants who has just
evened the score with his tattle-tale opponent. Since it was
given by such a tiny hand, Meridith scarcely felt the slap,
yet much to her delight, she knew that she had been properly
reprimanded.

Elmer's adversarial relationship to Meridith only seemed
to add zest to his life, and now that he had Palmer and me
together, his exuberance was boundless. He kept everyone
around him in an uproar of merriment by his outlandish
pranks. My husband and I told each other that we felt sorry
for all poor mortals who had no monkey to keep them
laughing.

Elmer was normally joyous, alert and intelligent. Yet on
rare occasions he could become deeply troubled. And at
such times he seemed to be totally withdrawn and
uncomprehending. When I was hospitalized for an extended
stay, the effect on Elmer was drastic. All the sparkle and fun
vanished.

My interlude at the hospital began with surgery. Palmer
came every day to see me, though it soon became evident
that it was not his wife but the monkey he was most
concerned about. The first thing I remember on coming out
from under the anesthetic was my husband sitting beside me
and saying "You've got to hurry and get well. Elmer just sits
there, hour after hour, with his eyes on the door waiting for
you."

The next day brought still another gloomy report. "I don't know what to do about Elmer. He eats almost nothing. He won't play. He won't even scold Meridith! Just watches that door and waits."

This was a strange state of affairs, I told myself. Here I was playing second fiddle to a monkey. Wasn't I the one who was supposed to get the sympathy? Nevertheless, I was as concerned as my husband.

Once Palmer brought Elmer and held him up outside my hospital window. While I could see them, the light was such that they could not see me. It certainly did no good for my peace of mind to observe that Elmer's once bright and lively eyes now held a blank, distracted look.

In spite of all the good hospital care and the cards and letters pouring in from kind parishioners, time for me dragged by with agonizing slowness. By the time the "No Visitors" sign was taken down from the door, my husband reported that "Elmer seems to have completely given up. I think he's convinced he'll never see you again. He no longer watches the door. But he doesn't do anything else either. He eats nothing, won't come out of his cage, takes no interest in anything." Then he concluded bluntly, "That monkey is going to die if you don't get home soon."

I therefore began to besiege the doctor to let me go home. "You need the rest," he argued. "You've been in a run-down condition for a long time and this operation has further weakened you. You'd better stay here and build up some strength while you can."

"I'll get my strength back," I replied almost frantically. "I promise. I'll stay in bed, I'll do anything you say. Only let me go home!"

"I sure can't understand why you're so eager to get out of here. Is this such a bad place?" the doctor inquired.

"No, it's a fine place," I replied. "But I need to be home." I was pretty certain he wouldn't have understood had I told him that I must get home to a grieving monkey. At any rate, I was finally allowed to leave the hospital several days early. Palmer hustled me through the formalities of leave-taking, got me into the car and sped homeward.

"I want you to go first thing to Elmer," he said, as though I needed to be told!

The monkey was a small black blob sitting motionless in his cage swing. He didn't even look toward the door when we entered.

I went to him, saying, "Elmer, I'm home. I'm home, Elmer. I'm home!"

He made no movement, no sign of recognition. His eyes were glazed, uncomprehending. I put my hands inside the cage and caressed him, and kept on talking to him.

At long last, his eyes began gradually to focus. He grasped one of my fingers with a tiny fist while he leaned against my hand and gazed out the window. He seemed to look far into the distance, and we could see brightness slowly kindle and then flame into comprehension in his eyes.

It was an expression that spoke eloquently: "She's home, she's really home. Everything is all right again."

As I fumbled for a handkerchief, my husband tightened his arm about me. He rubbed at his own tears with the back of his hand as he said, "Darned monkey!"

≫13≪

Rapscallion

Elmer seemed to snap back quickly to his usual happy, prankish self, in spite of his near-fatal grief experience. In fact, his recovery was more rapid than mine. Weeks went by when all I could do was recline on the sofa and try halfheartedly to read, or write thank-you notes. Mostly I just watched the monkey, who went all out to keep me entertained. After all, this was rare good fortune for him to have me there all the time, instead of forever dashing in and out, or sitting at the desk pouring over books and papers.

Actually, my slow physical recovery may have contributed more than a little to Elmer's emotional recovery. Had I left him alone soon after my return from the hospital, he might well have had a recurrence of total panic.

There was evidence he had not forgotten his harrowing experience. Every now and then, right in the middle of a seemingly carefree session of play, he left his toys to hop up onto the sofa beside me. With dark, serious eyes he looked me full in the face for a long, long time while he seemed to observe with wonderment my every feature. It was as though he must reassure himself, again and again, that I was really there.

Once satisfied, he tucked a thumb in his mouth, gave a contented grunt or two, then snuggled down against me to rest. As for me, I was stabbed with humility and something close to pain. It's a terrible thing to be the recipient of such devotion.

These occasions were only brief interludes, however. The rest of the time Elmer was in a delirium of happiness. I was there continually, Palmer came often to look in on us, and there was an almost steady stream of parishioners who brought wonderful gifts of food, much of which, to Elmer's great pleasure, he was allowed to sample. But even more than their gifts, the people themselves delighted him. He constantly chirruped, whistled, monkey-talked, did head stands and clowned for their entertainment. I was sure he even enjoyed having Meridith around, though he was still quick to tell her off if she interfered with him in any way.

One summer day after I was improved in health, a caller came who needed uninterrupted attention. Therefore, I took Elmer out to the enclosed back porch and anchored him by his long leash to a heavy iron kettle. He had progressed from the iron skillet to the kettle since he had become such a sturdy little guy he could now pull the skillet. I gave him some toys and left him alone to play and explore the porch. He scolded a little when I firmly closed the screen door between the porch and the kitchen and returned to my guest in the living room.

Considerable time had elapsed when I finally let my caller out the front door. I went back inside and stood contemplating the recent conversation. Suddenly I was startled by a wild flurry of movement, and Elmer shot past me like a miniature whirling dervish.

He flicked me a mirthful, devilish gleam of the eye as he swished by. Then he madcapped round and round the room, over and under the furniture, and up and down the doors and windows. Every move of his prancing, smart-alecky little body and his tiny, smirking face told me, "See, I got back inside all by myself. Ha, ha, ha! Fooled you, didn't I!"

And fooled me he had. He had unfastened his leash, I don't know how. And he had managed to open that stout wooden screen door. To do this he would have had to climb up to the latch, brace his legs against the door jamb, turn the latch handle away from him, then while holding it in this position, somehow pull open the heavy door. But that was my Elmer! So I laughed with him and told him what a rascal he was. And if possible, he was even more pleased with himself.

That summer I took Elmer for visits to the annual two-week Daily Vacation Bible School. He played to capacity crowds, having been scheduled ahead of time to appear on Tuesday of each week.

A class on that first Tuesday was a sampling of our visits. The room was jammed with wiggly, excited youngsters when I walked in with Elmer sitting perky and expectant on my shoulder. Even though most of the children knew us, the teacher made a polite introduction anyway, and then asked them if they wouldn't like to say good morning to us. Of course this was all those small bodies of compressed energy needed to explode. Their response was prompt, loud and shrill:

"Good morning, Rev-rund Gertrude! Good morning, El-mer!"

Elmer made no whistled greeting in reply. All this shrill noise was just too much. Whereas he had been sitting on my shoulder while clinging casually to a lock of my hair, now his tail and two arms went tightly around my neck and he tucked his head under my chin.

One little boy said, "He looks scared."

I said, "Yes, he is scared. And it's my fault. I should have told you that when there are many people around and they make a lot of noise, he gets frightened. He's a smart little monkey, and he knows what 'good morning' means, but this time he was so confused by hearing you all speak at once that he just didn't understand."

I explained to them the need to be very quiet and gentle to win Elmer's friendship, and that I believed this was true for all small animals. Elmer was also afraid of many reaching hands, I told them. He liked to be the one to make the first advances. And he was terrified if he was alone in his cage and then found himself surrounded by strangers. He'd had bad experiences when some people surrounded his cage and jabbed sticks at him just to hear him scream and scold. They thought it was funny, but it was not at all funny to a little monkey who couldn't get away, and who was so tiny that his only means of defense were his teeth.

By now the children were models of quiet decorum and eyed Elmer with the utmost sympathy. Elmer, in turn, began to relax. He soon loosened his grip on my neck and sat up and grinned. I took this occasion of the grin to point out those sharp eyeteeth.

"Elmer is a friendly little guy," I explained, "but when he gets very frightened, like when someone is poking at him through the wires of his cage, he will first scold as hard as he can. Then if that someone insists on poking a finger at him, that finger gets bitten."

The children were now all smiling back at the monkey. Though they scarcely took their eyes off Elmer, I sensed that they absorbed every word I said.

Actually, it was the adults who most often ignored my advice about pointing sticks and fingers at the monkey. They would not believe that anything that tiny and innocent looking could suddenly, in a flash of fear and fury, puncture a finger clear to the bone.

I did not tell this to the children, but I had a vivid recollection of a woman who once brought her small child to see the monkey. At least the child was her excuse. She permitted the little girl to stick her fingers into Elmer's cage even after I had asked her not to allow it. Therefore, as I saw Elmer grow fearful and agitated at all that darting, jabbing and squealing, I took the little girl firmly in hand and held her away from the cage. But I couldn't very well take the woman in hand when she did the same thing. So Elmer bit her finger!

After that the woman was considerably subdued but seemed resentful, though goodness knows, she'd been warned.

Anyway, I took her to the doctor, not wanting to run even the slightest chance of an infection. This doctor's attitude differed markedly from the one at the university clinic. I was cheered as he chuckled and joked while he tended the finger, though the woman remained glum and unsmiling. He told us not to worry, the tiny puncture would heal in no time. Afterward I paid the bill and took her back to the parsonage where she and the child then got into her car and drove away.

This experience was in the back of my mind while I tried to tell the children about the importance of being gentle, not only with Elmer, but with all animals. I even managed to get in a plug for being kind to people.

But the children were much more interested in this one small monkey in particular than in all living creatures in general. By now Elmer had lost his fear and was clowning and trying to stand on his head on my shoulder. The youngsters, not wanting to frighten him again, were holding their hands tight over their mouths in an effort to suppress their giggles. I told them I was sure Elmer knew now that they were his friends, so it would be all right for them to laugh out loud. In fact, he was deliberately trying to make them laugh.

So the children laughed out loud. Then they asked innumerable questions about what he liked to eat, what kind of toys he played with, and what all he could do. I answered as best I could and then let him demonstrate one of the things he liked to do. I called for a sheet of paper and a pencil, then transferred Elmer from my shoulder to the teacher's desk and told him the boys and girls would like to see him write. He was glad to oblige.

The monkey took that pencil, looked it over critically, felt the tip, smelled the eraser. Then, seeming satisfied, he hunched over and set to work scribbling on the paper with great industry. As usual, he tried to appear unaware of his watchers though his small back fairly exuded importance and his bright eyes darted quick, sideways glances at his young audience. The children were properly impressed.

Elmer had finished writing and was back on my shoulder when a quiet little girl raised her hand for recognition.

"Did you say Elmer came from South America?" she inquired politely.

I said, "Yes, he came from Brazil in South America."

Then this little girl informed me with prim earnestness, "I'm also going to bring someone to visit Bible School next week. It's my aunt, and she's from Australia."

To this small child, it would seem that an aunt from Australia and a monkey from South America were of equal importance.

Just before time to leave for our next class, a little redheaded boy missing a front tooth wanted to know if the monkey lost his baby teeth like kids. I told them that Elmer's teeth were very much like theirs, except that his eyeteeth were much sharper. And yes, as a matter of fact, Elmer had just lost a baby tooth.

The children clamored to know what the baby tooth looked like, and could they see it.

"No," I replied. "Elmer considers that tooth his very own treasure. He's so fond of it that he keeps it hidden, and even I can't find it. Oh, every now and then he brings it out and shows it to me. But he won't let me touch it. It's tiny and sparkling white, and Elmer examines it for a long time. Then he plays with it. He tosses it up in the air and catches it, or throws it from one hand to the other. Then all of a sudden it's gone. But he never lets me know when or where he hides it."

The newspapers now and then omitted church news, such as who was coming to speak. But they never failed to report an appearance by Elmer.

This time both the town's papers carried articles about the monkey. One was headed, "Monkey Elmer Guest at Bible School." It then went on to tell details of the event, and even reported that Elmer had lost a tooth.

≫14≪

No Comment

Because being separated from me had such a devastating effect on Elmer, he and I made a good many automobile trips together, trips that I might otherwise have taken by public conveyance at less time and expense. The longest journey was the one taken during our second year at St. Helens, when the monkey and I circled a large part of the nation. This extended trip was possible since Palmer and I now served the same church, and one of us could go away occasionally and leave the work to the other.

The imminent arrival of my husband's grandchild was the impetus for this long trip. Meridith was now with her husband at Wright Patterson Air Force Base near Dayton, Ohio. Palmer felt that it would be a good thing for me to be there when she and the baby came home from the hospital.

One day while we were discussing the trip, my husband grinned and tweaked Elmer as he said, "How do you suppose this guy will take to a brand new baby?"

I replied that I didn't know, but promised to report on it as soon as we got home.

That trip idea grew and grew. Not only would I visit folks between the west coast and Dayton, Ohio, but since Dayton was so near the east coast, I would naturally go on to Washington, D. C. to see my son Glen, his wife and my ten-month-old grandson Sheldon. They were there while Glen studied for his Master's degree at George Washington University. By the time I had gone that far, of course, it would be too late in the season to go back by the way I had come, because of the risk of wintry storms and icy roads. Therefore I might as well go to see other friends and relatives while taking the long way home: down the east coast, across the south, then up the west coast.

In preparation for the journey, I got rid of the car that had given me so much trouble on the way home from Texas. I traded it in on a little red and white Metropolitan. This was one of the first small cars to come out, and it seemed just made for Elmer and me. The seat fitted me perfectly, and I didn't have to stretch to see out or to reach the pedals. There was plenty of room for Elmer's cage on the seat beside me. When Palmer or someone else rode along, the cage could easily be transferred to the small seat in back.

I'm certain the makers of this car never dreamed of anyone sleeping in it. However, I discovered that I could simply remove a bolt from the hinged part of the right seat, drop the back down even with the rear seat, then let down the door to the trunk, which opened inside the car. And presto, there was plenty of room for a blanket-bed on which I could stretch out and be comfortable.

This would be a great way to save on expenses, I told my husband. Instead of paying for motel rooms, Elmer and I could sleep in the car on those nights between visitation points.

Palmer, holding the monkey in the crook of his arm, stroked him slowly as he replied, "Well, I don't know about that. Don't you think Elmer will be scared of the dark?"

I laughed at my husband's sly sense of humor. The question really meant, "Do you think it's safe for a woman to spend nights alone in her car?" Still, while he thought Elmer might be afraid, it didn't seem to occur to him that his wife might not be completely fearless on a dark night in a strange place.

We left St. Helens on the fifth of October, and our first stop was in Northwestern Washington for a week's stay at the farm with Paul and his wife, Evelyn. There Elmer ran in the soft grass, pranced in the skittering October leaves and, since we had extended the length of his leash, even climbed high into the giant walnut tree in front of the house.

Of course, since this was a dairy farm, we took the monkey to the barn to see the long rows of cows and the little calves in their pens. However, the bedlam of bawling, mooing and banging of stanchions was so overwhelming to the small monk that he clung to me with all his might, and shrank from any contact with these terrible creatures. He wouldn't even have anything to do with the dog or the cats, since they too were a part of the fearsome barn scene.

I realized too late what a foolish thing it had been to take Elmer so suddenly into all that noise and confusion. He could have taken the whole barnful of animals in stride, had he been introduced to them gradually.

Apart from the barn area, Elmer was heady with excitement over all the things to be explored. In the house there were dark closets to be investigated, high doors and windows to climb, cupboards to be examined, drawers to be pried open, and numerous locks to be inspected.

The day we were to leave, he was working on the old-fashioned square lock on the partly open door between the kitchen and dining room. Paul, Evelyn and I had lingered over lunch and were studying my road maps.

As Paul pushed back some dishes and rattled open a map, he glanced over his shoulder at Elmer, who clung to the edge of the door with his feet and one hand while he thoughtfully fingered the keyhole with the other.

"I hope," my son said, "that Elmer gets that wobbly lock fixed. My wife's been after *me* to do it!"

A moment later there was a shriek from the monkey and then a continuous stream of terrified screaming. Elmer, no longer clinging to the edge of the door, seemed to be whirling wildly around and around the lock. We all rushed to him, and I tried to hold him steady while I yelled to the others above the noise, "His finger's stuck in the keyhole!"

I spoke soothingly to the monkey, "There, there now, Elmer. You just hold still and we'll get your finger loose in no time."

But none of us could think of how to do it. That finger was really jammed tight. Then Evelyn had an inspiration. She rushed to the kitchen table and came back with a gob of butter. She smeared it liberally around Elmer's finger and over the keyhole area.

As I continued to hold firmly to the struggling monkey, I also worked his finger gently. Suddenly he was free! Still crying and frightened, but free. I put salve on the bruised finger, and each of us stroked and sympathized with him.

Soon, Elmer stopped his prolonged crying and only whimpered occasionally to remind us of his bad experience. Then, from a certain gleam in his eyes, we understood that as the salve was to his finger, so was the sympathy to his soul. He liked them both!

Paul laughed, then exclaimed as he looked at the clock, "Gosh, I've got work to do!" In one motion he threw on his cap and jacket and banged out through the door.

An hour later, when the car was all packed and Elmer and I were ready to leave, my son came running back from the barn to say goodbye. Elmer sat in his cage at my feet, so Paul carried it around and placed it on the right side of the seat, while I slid in behind the steering wheel.

Paul tickled Elmer's stomach through the cage wires as he admonished me, "Mother, you better keep this guy away from those locks in your motel rooms. There probably won't be any butter there!"

I pointed to the pillow and blankets in the baggage compartment as I replied, "We're going to sleep in the car."

"What?" My son at first looked incredulous. Then his eyes twinkled, his lips twitched, and his shoulders wriggled while he gazed off into the distance. When he finally looked back at me, he broke into uncontrolled, teasing laughter.

"Now, Mom, I want you to make me a promise. Promise that you'll send me a postcard every single night that you and Elmer sleep in this car."

Though I promised, it was plain to see that he didn't expect to get any such cards.

Since it had been well into the afternoon before we left Paul's, it was rather late before I even looked for a place to stop for the night. By the time we reached Yakima on the east side of the mountains, it was dark. I had hoped to find a tourist park where I could stay for the night, but I couldn't find one.

Soon we were out of town and into lonely, open country. There didn't even seem to be any farm houses along the highway. Finally, I glimpsed some fenced-in buildings off to the left with plenty of space between the board fence and the road. So I pulled over next to the fence and told Elmer these were our accommodations for the night.

I took the monkey out of his cage and we ran around the car a few times for exercise, then I peered out over our location. The night sky was beautiful, with multitudes of stars riding serenely above us. But here below, all was dark loneliness. The buildings proved to be, not dwellings, but a county fairgrounds complex. There wasn't even an echo of the animals, people, confusion and carnival excitement of the last county fair. It was strange, eerie, like another world.

Elmer also peered around at our shadowy surroundings, while he clung tight to my neck and asked questions. He couldn't understand what on earth we were doing at a place like this so late at night. Palmer had been right. Elmer didn't like it, and to tell the truth, neither did I. But I had told that son of mine that we were going to sleep in the car, and sleep in the car we would.

I let the seat down, unrolled blankets and was soon in my bed. Elmer was beside me, cuddled down in his own bed in the open cage. The monkey was tired, so he quickly flipped the covers over himself, sighed, tucked his thumb in his mouth, and went through his go-to-sleep ritual.

But he didn't sleep much. He was troubled by the alternating silence of the country night and the noise from passing traffic. When a truck went by, it was like an alien thing that invaded our stillness, shook us with its terrible roar, and then left us to the waiting darkness. Elmer was insulted by the noise, and said so, but he was also distrustful of that great silence that stood stock-still around us after the racket was gone.

We were also upset by the lights of vehicles coming over the hill. They blazed directly down upon us and seemed to deliberately pick us out. I managed to put some make-shift covers over the car windows which helped, but only a little.

Finally, after an unusually long stretch of silence, the monkey seemed to have fallen into a light sleep, and I was beginning to relax.

Then an automobile blazed over the hill, gradually slowed its speed, and came to a stop at the edge of the road only a few yards from us.

I grabbed the hammer I always carried in the car and sat up. Simultaneously Elmer sprang from his bed and wrapped himself tight around my neck.

Thus we waited.

There were low, masculine voices. Doors opened and banged shut. Shadowy figures got out of the car, moved about, then got back in. Finally the auto turned and sped away. Elmer and I were again alone in the night.

I fell back limply, but Elmer still hung on to my neck. I peeled him away gently while telling him that everything was okay and now we must really go to sleep. Once again he went through his go-to-sleep ceremony, but he still slept very little. Time and again I dropped into a partial doze, only to be awakened by tiny hands fumbling under my covers and patting me, feeling all over my face and hands. Elmer needed to reassure himself that I was there. Each time I stroked and soothed him and returned him to bed.

At length, when the monkey patted me back to full consciousness, I was horrified to hear shuffling steps approaching from the rear.

I sprang upright, hammer in hand, while the monkey locked himself around my neck. Immobilized with fear, I didn't even try to see out the back window. I just sat there waiting while the steps came nearer and nearer.

They stopped and advanced, stopped and advanced. The nearer they came, the more it seemed to me there were at least two people back there. I wondered in panic if the men who had stopped their car out by the road had circled around somehow and were walking back.

Those stealthy steps were almost alongside the car when I suddenly came to life. I slid from my bed to the driver's seat and turned the ignition key. Then I threw back the cover from the windshield and turned on the lights while my shoeless foot felt for the gas pedal.

At the same instant there was a heavy commotion outside the car, and then a large dark form stood for a moment poised in the sheet of light. It snorted and tore off into the night.

It was a horse!

I turned off the ignition and the lights and collapsed back onto the bed with Elmer still around my neck. He hadn't made a sound through this whole episode, but now he began to croon gently in my ear, his way of trying to comfort both of us. He seemed to say, "It's all right. That big old scary thing is gone now." I'm sure he sensed my relief as I stroked him and put him back in bed.

At last dawn began to shimmer against the horizon. Elmer hopped out from under his covers and came again to pat me and to kiss my face with his small monkey kisses. He had to make certain that I knew it was morning.

I got up and soon had the blankets folded and the Metro back in order. With Elmer on his leash, we got out to exercise in the crisp morning air. He didn't much care for the stiff, dry grass, so he scooted up a fence post and ran along the top of the board fence. I held the end of the leash and trotted along beside him. Elmer grinned happily down at me and I laughed back. This wasn't a bad place at all with the sun coming up.

There was one thing more to do before driving away. I wrote a card to my son Paul to tell him that Elmer and I had slept in the car that night.

It was the only such card he would get.

The weather was bright and beautiful and the Metro sped effortlessly over mountains and across plains. There were no such problems as I'd had with the Ford on my way home from Texas.

The monkey and I stayed at motels between visiting points. No more sleeping out for us! We stopped to see relatives and friends in Cheyenne, Wyoming, and in western

Iowa, then went on to my parents' farm near Winterset, Iowa, where we would stay until I got a call from Meridith's husband that the new baby had arrived.

I savored this time of being with my father and mother and of again experiencing October in Iowa, with its wide fields of crackling corn stalks and its long fence rows red with sumac.

Elmer was also happy. Some of the time he just rocked quietly in his swing. At other times he put on a regular whirling dervish display of acrobatic stunts. And much of the time he whistled, trilled, chattered, and made elaborate efforts to hide the fact that he simply reveled in the attention of my parents.

He was enraptured the day my father came in and handed him a mirror with a handle. How he loved mirrors! This was an especially wonderful mirror because that slender handle made it much easier to use than the one he was occasionally allowed to have at home. He could easily grasp the handle by one hand and have the other free for exploration of his features. Therefore, as he began his mirror antics, he became completely absorbed and oblivious.

Well, not quite. He still remembered, periodically, to take a quick look around to see if his audience was still with him.

He arched his eyebrows and grinned and grimaced while he fingered an eye or pulled at an ear. In addition to seeing what kinds of awful faces he could make, he also wanted to know what was back of his eyes and inside his ears. Most of all he wanted to find out what his insides were like from his teeth clear down to his toes, so he began a systematic investigation. First he felt and studied each tooth, then he examined his tongue, sticking it out, pulling it in, lifting it with his hand to see underneath.

The alarming part, for me at any rate, was when he got to the tonsils and throat. Here he yanked and twisted his tongue from side to side in order to increase his view. As he strained to see ever farther down his throat, he pulled harder and harder on his tongue until I feared he would tear it out.

At first, my parents were delighted at Elmer's clowning but now they, too, were becoming worried. So, knowing that there was no end to his self-examination, I confiscated the mirror to the tune of loud and shrill protests. Above his scolding, I explained to my folks that Elmer's ruthless yanking at his tongue was why I seldom allowed him to have a mirror. Yet I had to admit that I had never known him to really injure himself.

"He must be made of elastic," my father commented with a chuckle.

"Yes," I responded, "but those fingernails aren't, and they're so long I'm afraid he'll gash his tongue with them. He's got to have them clipped right away." This was a task I had put off too long, mainly because the monkey objected so strenuously to the process.

Later that day, I scooped Elmer up and told him the time had come when his nails had to be clipped. Holding a tiny foot in a firm grasp, I clipped away while Elmer jerked and twisted and screamed to the high heavens.

My back was to my dad and mother, but I suddenly became aware that the silence behind was almost as loud as Elmer's hullabaloo. Even my dad was stony silent, and that was bad, as I knew from past experience. They were both on Elmer's side and I was in high disfavor.

But what could I do? This little monkey did not live in the forest where he could wear his nails down by climbing trees. If they went uncut, not only might he hurt himself, but they would curve under and become painful.

I worked on doggedly while Elmer continued to twist and turn and split the air with cries that he was being tortured. Finally I started on the last fingernail.

Then it happened!

The monkey let out a shriek that went straight through the ceiling. I saw with horror that blood was flowing from a tiny, black finger.

I told Elmer over and over how sorry I was, and tried desperately to comfort him. Added to my distress and misery was the knowledge of my parents' disapproval. I felt like a little girl again just before a spanking. And as in the days of childhood, I somehow felt I had it coming.

Elmer's shriek had brought my father and mother both up out of their chairs. Now my dad stood over me and broke his silence. "*Gosh all-mighty*, Gertrude, you ought to be more careful with that little feller!"

My mother, strong on action but never one for many words, hurried away and soon came back with some sort of medication and bandage material. She took Elmer from me and crooned gently as she set to work doctoring the cut finger.

Elmer's cries slackened while she worked, then turned to intermittent sobs. Soon he stopped crying altogether, except now and then when he remembered how bad it had all been. Then he puckered up his lips, whimpered and snuggled against her.

I myself began to feel better when Elmer darted a look at me and I caught a flash of smug satisfaction in his eyes. All this time my dad had been standing near, watching the proceedings. When he too saw that certain gleam in Elmer's eyes, he burst out laughing and exclaimed, "Why, that little devil! He's enjoying this!"

My mother looked up and smiled at me, and I felt forgiven. I felt even more forgiven after she gave the monkey back to me, and he snuggled up with his arms around my neck. He complained a little, but when I soothed him he was content. I was sure he knew I hadn't meant to hurt him.

Of course, the bandage didn't stay on Elmer's finger for long. Back in the cage he just had to take it off. He unrolled it, studied it with great concentration, smelled it, tasted the salve, and rolled it up again. Then he carefully scrutinized the hurt finger, but by now it had stopped bleeding and no longer seemed so bad.

However, the little rascal had a good thing going for himself and wasn't about to give it up. After that, each time my mother came anywhere near him, Elmer quivered his lips as though he were about to start sobbing his heart out, then shoved his finger out for her to examine. And each time my mother's blue eyes softened and smiled as she stooped to take his tiny hand and examine the finger.

We had been at my parents' only a few days when the phone call came from Meridith's husband, Jerry. The baby had arrived early that morning of October twenty-ninth. All was well and mother and baby would be home from the hospital in five days. That would be November third. I told Jerry I would arrive on that date.

My father and mother were disappointed to have Elmer and me leave so soon. However, I explained that Meridith and her husband were both pretty young, that Meridith had never cared for a newborn baby before, and that she would really need help when she got home with the baby. Therefore, with visions of being anxiously awaited, I pushed hard all day toward Dayton. I even passed by the home of a friend I had fully expected to visit, and only took time enough at noon for Elmer and me to have a quick lunch and a brief run for exercise.

Having never been in Dayton before, it took some extra time to find the address I was looking for. Nevertheless, by 6:30 p.m., with Elmer on my shoulder, I was hurrying up a long flight of stairs to their apartment. It was a good thing we made it this soon, I was thinking. The evening of a woman's first day home with her new baby was usually a trying time, but here I was, ready and eager to ease the situation with all my motherly arts.

I took the last two steps with a bound. The monkey jiggled on my shoulder as I hit the landing and drew up in front of the door. I lifted my hand to knock, and then let it fall limply as I saw the sheet of paper labeled "MOM" stuck in the door. I glanced at the message but didn't believe what I had seen until I read it aloud to Elmer.

"We have gone to a friend's house to watch TV. Be back around midnight."

I entered the apartment in a daze and sank down on the small sofa in the kitchen-living room. Elmer slid from my shoulder to the floor and tugged at the end of his leash as he went for a brief round of exploration. Then he came back and stood erect at my feet and looked intently up at me while his dark eyes flared questions, "What are we doing in this strange house? Why aren't there any people here?"

I said to him, "I don't know, Elmer. I'm just as bewildered as you are."

Then suddenly I leaned back and laughed, long and loud. "You know what, Elmer? I've just learned something. I'm not indispensable, after all!"

Brightness rose in the monkey's eyes, and he flipped a couple of somersaults. He wasn't going to worry about this situation if I didn't.

While I fixed Elmer and me a bit of supper, I reflected that, while it may not have been exactly the wise thing to do, it was good that Meridith felt well enough to go out for the evening on her first day home from the hospital. Also, I reminded myself, she and Jerry probably expected that I would not arrive till around midnight, as I might have done had I taken the trip more leisurely.

The apartment was very small, and there wasn't really any place for Elmer and me to sleep. Therefore, I used the extra time to go room hunting. After considerable driving around and peering at signs under dim lights, I finally found a room just a little over a block from the apartment. Here I unloaded the car, washed Elmer and changed his shirt and diaper, got myself freshened up, then sat and cuddled the monkey while I wrote a letter to Palmer. After that we went back to Meridith's and Jerry's place. There was still no one around, so Elmer lay in his cage and slept while I wrote another letter.

I heard the baby's thin wail at the same moment I became aware of steps on the stairs. I sprang up to meet them. After our brief flurry of greetings, I bent over the baby basket and a tiny beating fist closed around one of my fingers.

"He's wonderful," I murmured. "What's his name?" In the excitement of Jerry's phone call I'd forgotten to ask.

They told me his name was Dougie. "At least we call him Dougie," Jerry said. "Jerald Douglas is too big a name for such a little tyke."

Right now Dougie was miserable, and he was crying. Also, his mother looked tired. I decided they needed me after all.

The baby lay in the glare of a bright light, and I wondered if these inexperienced kids had kept him under lights all evening. I promptly set to work helping them get Dougie away from the light and making him comfortable. When the little one was quiet and resting, I remembered my husband's admonition to let him know what Elmer thought of the baby.

We had temporarily forgotten the monkey. Now awake, bright-eyed and eager, he clung to the wires of his cage and shook it vigorously for attention. When I took him out, Meridith reached to touch him, but he drew back and sassed her, though he looked happy while doing it. He was not about to let her forget that she was his avowed adversary.

I don't know what we expected Elmer's reaction to be toward Dougie, but when I held him over the basket, he peered down gravely at the sleeping infant and made not the slightest sound. During our whole stay there, Elmer's manner toward the baby was the same: grave, brooding, noncommittal.

Our Dayton visit went fast. I let Elmer run and play when we were in our room down the street. At the apartment he was content to stay in his cage and watch everything that went on. He seemed to take a keen interest in watching me while I cooked, cleaned and created makeshift shelves of apple boxes for groceries. Meridith and Jerry had to live on a small salary, while at the same time they were pretty unskilled in the art of housekeeping and making do with little. This was an area in which I felt competent to help, as well as assisting in the care of the baby.

On the day we took our departure, Meridith was bathing the baby in her sparkling clean kitchen. I leaned over to kiss naked little Dougie while Elmer took one more long, silent look.

Then we were off. At Glen's home in Washington, D. C., Elmer's response to my ten-month-old grandson, Sheldon, was completely different from what it had been to the new baby. He trilled and whistled and constantly stretched his arms through the wires of the cage toward the toddler. Here was someone who reached and chattered right back at him. There was no silent pondering here. This was a time to laugh and celebrate! (There would be equal laughter and celebration with Baby Dougie when he became a few months older.)

Two months and four days from the day of departure, Elmer and I arrived back at St. Helens.

"Well, what did Elmer think of my new grandson?" Palmer inquired.

I described all that silent pondering, and then told my husband that I believed Elmer was profoundly impressed with his grandson though he made no comment.

Palmer chuckled and suddenly switched the subject.

"Things sure were dull around here without you and Elmer," he said, and then added with a sly twinkle, "Especially without Elmer!"

⇒15⇐

Men Only

My husband and I asked for a transfer from the church at St. Helens after only two years. It was not that we did not enjoy operating as a team. Nor were we unhappy with the people we served. Far from it! But we had had this time to work together and in the process to solidify our marriage. Now we felt it was time to keep our pre-marriage agreement to pastor separate churches. Meridith, with her baby, was again living at home. She could be housekeeper for her father.

We had not anticipated the reaction our request for two churches precipitated. The district superintendent we first approached informed Palmer and me in no uncertain terms that the place for a minister's wife was either in the parsonage or at her husband's side at all times. To bolster this argument, he extolled at great length the virtues of certain women in both his near and distant ancestry who had stayed home and served the Lord by serving their husbands.

No, he personally would have no church for me, and he felt certain that the other superintendents and the bishop would agree with him. Never mind that the denomination he served had fully ordained me a minister in my own right. I was now, as far as he was concerned, first and foremost a minister's *wife*. Period!

Anyway, he continued, most of the church positions were already filled for that year. Certainly they didn't have two parishes sitting side by side just waiting for a ministerial couple, and furthermore, he wasn't about to contribute to the breakup of a home by appointing us to two churches several miles apart.

Then he finished with his clincher. "I don't know of a single congregation anywhere on my district that would even *have* a woman preacher!"

In defense of my denomination, I must say that this is the only church leader I ever encountered with such an extreme attitude toward women ministers. Fortunately, this particular superintendent did not have the final say about placements and our bishop and the other district superintendents were much more broad minded.

The man had been right about one thing, however. There really weren't many churches in need of pastors that year. In the end, Palmer and I were appointed to two churches about 250 miles down the coast from our present location.

Palmer's church would be at North Bend, a parish comparable to the one we were leaving, while I was given, apologetically, a small parish in the town of Gardiner, about twenty-five miles north of his.

The superintendent of this district told me frankly I would find very little at Gardiner except opportunity. It appeared he wasn't even certain about the opportunity. For years, he said, no one sent there had been able to accomplish much. He pointed out that he himself had once spent several weeks of work on that parish without making any progress.

"You are to be their last chance," he concluded. "If nothing happens this year, the church will be officially closed."

I don't know why I wasn't discouraged. I simply accepted the appointment and went back to St. Helens to pack, help prepare for our final services and tell our friends goodbye.

It was a sunny, late afternoon in June when I slowed the car to a stop in the small town of Gardiner.

To my right arose the scrape and whine of a sawmill that sat on a strip of land between the road and the Umqua River. Far out, the river blended into the Pacific to form a panoramic sheet of water that shimmered away into a purple hazed horizon.

My attention, however, was centered mainly on the battered old church to my left. Its front doors hung listlessly ajar, and it was encircled by weeds and tall grass. There was no sign of a welcoming committee.

The moving van had already pulled up at the equally dilapidated dwelling back of the church. Blue hydrangeas stood up out of the weeds to lean against its weathered front porch.

I took Elmer from the car and went over to the two truckers who stood viewing the scene with uncertainty. They were both loyal members of the church I had just left. "Are you sure you want us to unload your things *here*?" one of them asked. "We'll gladly take you back to St. Helens if you want."

Right then I felt almost like going back, especially when we found that, unlike the church, the parsonage doors were securely locked.

But I had reached the point of no return. The movers leaned against their truck while I returned Elmer to the car and went in search of a key.

I assumed it was held by someone nearby so I went to a neighboring home and knocked on the door. Introducing myself to the lady who finally appeared, I asked if she could tell me how to get the parsonage key.

With a seeming lack of interest, the woman gave me the name of someone in the nearby town of Reedsport whom she thought might have it. Then she offered me the use of her phone.

After a time of waiting, a beautiful young woman came with the key. Her blue eyes were kind but during that brief stop she seemed preoccupied, and said little.

The downstairs of the old parsonage was as decrepit as the outside. However, the upstairs was a pleasant surprise. It had been made into a cozy apartment consisting of hall, living room, kitchen, bedroom and bath. This would give me sufficient room in which to live and work.

Elmer sat on my shoulder and looked about with immense curiosity, and a tinge of apprehension. Our living room and kitchen opened together into one big room with cheerful paint and wallpaper. The windows looked out on a tree-covered mountainside. A row of houses sat at the foot of the mountain, while a few others were tucked higher up into its side.

I put Elmer's cage on a table by the kitchen window. From there the monkey trilled and chattered, and occasionally threw little questioning sounds at me, while the men lugged boxes and furniture up the steep stairs and put them in place.

After the movers left, the excitement that had so far kept me going suddenly evaporated. Was my coming here a terrible mistake? It seemed pretty obvious that no one wanted me. Elmer soaked up my mood and now sat silent in his swing, regarding me with big, questioning eyes.

We both jumped when the phone rang. It was Palmer calling to check up on us.

"Elmer and I are just fine," I told him. My husband sounded happy. There was no need to pass on my gloom. We agreed that since we would both be busy unpacking and getting settled, we would not see each other before late Sunday. Yes, Palmer said, he and Meridith and Dougie had been welcomed with much fanfare, food and friendliness.

His comment about food reminded me not only of our lack of a welcome, but that Elmer and I had not eaten for some time. The monkey especially needed something besides those bits of orange and carrot in his cage.

While I opened cardboard boxes in search of something to eat, Elmer seemed to have decided that he would have to cheer me up. He began to grin, caper, and clown, all the while keeping a sharp eye out to see my reaction. I laughed a little in spite of myself.

Then, without conscious volition, I suddenly turned from the clutter of unpacking, put Elmer on my shoulder and ran downstairs to the hydrangeas.

Wading among the weeds, I picked a blossom for Elmer and then talked to him while I gathered a bouquet for the apartment.

"This hydrangea bush must have been here for a long time," I said, "and as soon as the weeds are cut from around it and the soil tended, its blossoms will nod their blue beauty to all who pass by."

"The church is like the hydrangeas," I told him. Even now it held a faded loveliness and whispers of better times.

"You will see, Elmer, a handful of people, a few repairs and paint, and this place will come to life again. I have faith that this will be!"

Back upstairs, I placed the bouquet in the middle of the table's disarray. The hydrangeas were to be my reminder that all was going to be well with me and the church. Elmer and I ate and were cheered.

By the end of the week, however, my faith was being tested. Elmer looked at me with puzzled, dark eyes and chirruped questions while I busied myself with more unpacking and preparations for the Sunday service. Moving day had been Wednesday, and the three days that followed were probably the most uninterrupted days we had ever experienced. The monkey did not like it. He preferred interruptions.

The district superintendent had given me the name of a person who could be contacted if necessary. As no one had contacted me, I phoned Jim Worthington to inquire about the hour for the Sunday morning service.

"Will it be at eleven o'clock," I asked, "or do you meet earlier during the summer?"

There was a long pause at the other end of the line. Then Mr. Worthington said, "I guess 11:00 will be as good a time as any." After another pause he added, "My wife and I will make some phone calls. But I can't guarantee that you'll have a congregation."

There were eleven people at church that first Sunday. I was later to learn that this was a big crowd compared to attendance at previous services. Jim and his wife must have done some persuasive phoning.

I don't quite know what I expected those people to be like—perhaps old, beaten and bedraggled like the church building. But I was pleasantly surprised. The eleven sitting before me looked, for the most part, to be somewhere in their thirties or forties. They were neatly dressed, bright, crisp, even cheerful looking, though it seemed to me there might have been a bit of devilment lurking back of those cheerful faces, especially those of the men. I surmised it was probably at the expense of this woman minister. But never mind. Better to have friendly laughter at my expense than no laughter at all.

I don't remember much more about that first service, except that when it was over, all eleven members of my congregation came up to the apartment to see if I were comfortably situated.

And there they met Elmer.

The monkey was delighted. He apparently concluded that this was a delegation come solely on his behalf. It seemed that he was justified in that opinion since, from the moment of their entry, he was the one who definitely got the attention.

As usual he set out to make it worth their while. One by one he greeted each guest as he clung to a finger, looked up into a pair of eyes, and chattered enthusiastically. Then he went into his entertainment repertoire. Inside his cage he swung madly, first by two hands, then by one. Next he did his loop-the-loops, with both himself and his swing going at high speed. Then, tail anchored, he did his head stand while flashing a broad, upside-down grin at his cheering audience.

Then he sprang to the water bottle mounted in the corner of his cage. As he took a few swigs, he darted quick glances over his shoulder to see if everyone was properly impressed. It seemed they were, so he whistled and trilled while he dug about among his papers and toys for food. One could almost see the wheels turn in his clever little brain: if these people liked to see him drink water, surely they would also like to see him eat.

Soon he came up with half an orange, almost as big as he. He held it expertly in his two tiny hands while he alternately ate and monkey talked to the guests.

All at once he threw the orange down, having thought of something that would wow them even more.

Looking straight at me, then toward the refrigerator, the monkey uttered some special little sounds that I understood perfectly, having learned them long ago. In Elmer-talk, these syllables said, "Give me my bottle."

I obediently filled his doll bottle with milk, added the nipple, and handed it to him. The monkey sat straight up and downed the milk, tipping his head farther and farther back, all the while keeping a bright eye out for reactions. The Sunday morning congregation stood in the parsonage kitchen and laughed uproariously at this impish attention-grabber.

I accompanied the group downstairs as they took their leave. They paused at the foot of the porch steps, seeming a bit reluctant to go. The men looked over the place and agreed they'd better get busy and mow the weeds and grass right away.

The pretty lady who had brought the keys the day of my arrival said, "I'm really sorry I had to rush off that day, but I work in an office and I had to hurry back."

Jim Worthington spoke next. "I think we all want to apologize that no one was here to greet you when you came. I guess we were just put out at the district superintendent and the bishop for sending us a minister when we said we didn't want one. You see, we've been pretty discouraged here, and everybody just quit going to church. Our last minister left long before the end of the church year and it's been some time since we've had any kind of service. Until today." The others murmured assent. "Some of the ministers we've had in the past didn't seem to fit our needs at all. But, by golly, with you and Elmer here, we might be able to make a go of it yet! How about it, folks?"

I was gratified to hear enthusiasm in their voices. One of the women said, "I think we ought to bring our children next time and get a Sunday School started."

Another asked shyly if I would mind if they took turns bringing their children to see the monkey during the coming week.

So began our busy days at Gardiner. The wooden stairs to the apartment echoed with ascending and descending feet. Never again did we have three consecutive uninterrupted days. And never again would the entire Sunday congregation have fitted into the parsonage kitchen.

≫16≪

Waste and Destruction

The church school grew from zero that first Sunday to the point where, in less than three months, we were wondering what to do with all the children and youth, and making plans for an addition to the building.

Elmer made his first formal appearance at Sunday School on the second Sunday in September. The children had been told the previous week that when their attendance doubled, the monkey would come to visit. And so, on the very next Sunday, the attendance more than doubled.

Elmer came in on my shoulder, red shirted, bright eyed, and all set for adventure, though he was a bit wary at first. The children, and even the teachers, were an attentive audience while I extemporized about monkeys and people, and answered innumerable questions. Elmer, warming up to the crowd, demonstrated his writing ability and all the other attention-pleasers that came to his sharp, intuitive little mind. We left amid cheers and urgent requests for him to come back soon.

The occasion for Elmer's next Sunday School visit was Christmas Sunday. The children and I reasoned that if sheep, a donkey, and even camels were there at the time of Jesus's birth, surely the presence of a happy little Capuchin monkey would be acceptable in our celebration of His birthday.

At home, the steep stairs to our apartment were in continuous use. I was quite certain that many people, little and big, came more to see the monkey than me, though I basked in his popularity.

Elmer's welcome was usually one of trilling enthusiasm, but he was happiest of all when Palmer came. One sunny afternoon, when my husband's step sounded on the stairs, Elmer, who always knew those steps, shrilled a welcome all the way up and went into a frenzy of celebration. On this particular day Palmer hugged and kissed me rather perfunctorily.

Then he went straight to Elmer, took him out of his cage, and there ensued a glorious session of smooching, patting and hugging.

Oh, well, I told myself, it was my fault I didn't get that much attention from my husband. After all, *I* hadn't yelled, jumped up and down, and turned cartwheels on his arrival.

When Palmer and I settled down to talk, the monkey at first dominated the conversation. Now sitting on my husband's knee, now standing and clinging to his shirt front, he held forth with much eye to eye earnestness. I felt sure that if we could have understood, we would have heard him telling everything that had happened since Palmer's last visit. After getting all this talk out of his system, he carefully examined and admired Palmer's new tie and clasp. Then he went through all his pockets, taking out every single item to turn over, scrutinize, and finally replace. Last of all, he scampered to Palmer's shoulder and settled down to blissful relaxation and his usual examination of the black date book from the white shirt pocket. Occasionally he uttered a quiet monkey-talk aside.

At such times as this, the monkey exuded such utter satisfaction and contentment that my husband and I also felt lulled and rested. We smiled at each other over the head of our little monk, and for the present, all problems and struggles simply faded away. Tomorrow we would face them renewed.

I spent a large portion of my time each week calling on people, not only those at Gardiner and nearby Reedsport, but others along the coast and up and down the rivers. Some of these were long-inactive members while others were new in the community. When a church has become run down and the people discouraged, ministerial visits are vital.

At first I took Elmer with me and he loved it. But so did the people, so much so that Elmer got most of the attention and I was slowed in making my rounds. I soon discovered that it was best to leave the monkey in the car. That way, with luck he would not be discovered until I was ready to leave.

Summer went fast, and soon it was too damp and cold for my little South American monkey to stay in the car. How forlorn he looked that first day I left him home. I felt pangs of distress as I told him goodbye, and his crying followed me down the stairs.

Hours later when I entered the front door, I felt a small movement at my feet, and there was Elmer in a miserable little heap against the door jamb. It was cold in that gloomy downstairs hall and I had no idea how long he had waited there. Later I discovered that he had escaped from his parrot cage by unfastening the wire across one of the slots made for inserting bird seed. The door to the apartment had been left open, so Elmer, lonely and frightened, had gone downstairs to wait.

I picked up my chilled monkey and cuddled and soothed him. His lips worked and quivered exactly like those of a sobbing child. Elmer, however, only whimpered now and then. His sobbing was silent. Even though there were times when Elmer faked it if he just wanted to make me feel bad, this was real. Terribly real.

Upstairs, I let him snuggle on my shoulder and talked to him while tending to household chores and preparing our dinner. At length his mouth stopped quivering and he began to monkey-talk to me in mournful little tones, telling me, I'm certain, how awful it had been all alone in that big old creaky, scary house.

But now that everything was back to normal with light and warmth, the smell of cooking and the presence of his "mother," his mournfulness gradually gave way. He began the small reassurance ritual he always followed after a time of stress. He seemed to draw comfort to himself by consoling me, so he told me over and over in cozy, chirrupy tones that now all was well again.

After that I still had to leave Elmer alone, but I tried to leave him for only short intervals at first. He never did like it, but he began to play by himself, watch people below his second-story window, and get along quite well.

I reinforced his cage, and he didn't break out again for a long time. However, there came a day almost two years later, when after an extended absence, I went tearing up the stairs calling as usual, "Hello there, Elmer! I'm home! I'm home!" There was no reply from the upper floor, just a long deep silence.

At the living room door, I stopped in the middle of a "hello" and stared in stunned disbelief at a blizzard of jumbled papers, books, and garbage that covered my once neat living room-study and kitchen.

As I surveyed the scene, I was acutely aware that the cage was empty and the wire across a bird-seed slot dangled by one end. At the same time I sensed Elmer's presence. He was hiding out, of course, as he often did when he had been naughty. And today he was super-super naughty!

I was anything but happy. It was late afternoon and a meeting was scheduled to be held here that very evening. Right now not only was the entire surface of the floor profusely littered but so also was my desk, the kitchen table, the counter tops, and the sink. In the back of my mind lurked scripture passages about the waste and destruction brought about by the powers of evil. I was aggravated, but it struck my funny bone and I chuckled as I totaled up the ravages and depredation wrought by my own little devil.

Numerous pages had been torn from two prized books. The contents of a large filing drawer had been dumped out and well shuffled. A favorite framed picture lay on the floor with the back partially torn away. On the desk my appointment calendar had been industriously scribbled over with black pencil, while various books and papers were covered with monkey writing in red pencil punctuated by dashes of green.

The wastepaper basket by my desk had been partly emptied and its papers scattered, while the entire contents of the kitchen garbage bag had been removed. Tin cans, food wrappers and a bone lay among filing envelopes, books and papers. Both toys and dishes had been put to soak in the kitchen sink. A ball plugged the drain. Thank goodness, I thought, he had at least shut the water off.

It was evident that Elmer had been munching food while he indulged in all this mayhem, for bits of juicy apple and slimy banana were liberally mixed with all the litter on the desk, tables and floor. To make things even more sticky, a huge spool of cellophane tape had been completely unrolled from its dispenser and swirled grandly over the whole.

After my dazed inspection, I waded back to the desk and noticed that Elmer had taken the telephone receiver off the hook. As I replaced it, I discovered the crowning insult of all. That rascal had torn up next Sunday's sermon and tossed it disdainfully into the wastebasket!

This was pure sabotage, but what can one do to an absentee saboteur? Elmer had hit for cover the moment he heard me coming. He was well aware that he had been involved in illicit behavior, and he expected to get scolded. I looked for him but couldn't find him, so I scolded anyway. "Elmer, you naughty monkey! Why did you do this? No! No! You've been bad!" It was like talking to thin air, but I knew my small culprit was taking it all in from some hiding spot.

In the midst of my tirade, the telephone rang. When I answered, the person at the other end of the line said, "For goodness sakes, I've been trying practically all day to get you, and each time I got the busy signal."

While she was speaking, I looked up to see a cheeky little black visage appear above the top of the window drapes. It was plain that the smirking little demon had had himself one whale of a time, and despite all my scolding he was still in an unrepentant state of pure deviltry. I wanted to laugh but he expected indignation, so I gave him a stern look; whereupon the head disappeared from above the drapes.

My phone caller was saying, "I never did have such a time trying to phone you before. You surely must have been busy today."

I told her I was sorry she'd had so much trouble reaching me and that, "Well, yes, things have been pretty busy around here today."

It took me two hours of steady work to get the house back in some semblance of order. Such things as mixed up files and a torn up sermon would take more hours of time, but they would have to wait. Preparations still had to be made for that evening meeting, and I was supposed to do something about a mean little monkey. He had it coming and knew it. But all I could do was reprove and scold.

Elmer was no longer behind the drapes, and there was no time to make a thorough search. Therefore, I kept on talking to empty space about that naughty monkey, while I put a bright tablecloth on the table, got out dishes, and prepared refreshments for the guests.

Elmer continued to lay low and let me scold until finally I just ran down. Then suddenly there was a great rush and flurry, and Elmer shot out from somewhere to dash madly around and around the rooms, eyeing me all the while. The little imp was actually laughing at me and still savoring his wickedness.

What else could I do? I grabbed that small handful of hilarity and laughed with him. The time for scolding was past.

≫17≪

The Blizzard

Elmer loved having people around him and was the most sociable little fellow imaginable, yet he could sit alone for long periods of time and entertain himself with nothing more than a mere raveling of thread. He would feel it daintily, sniff it, taste it, put it around his wrists and fingers, and then wind it into all sorts of intricate curlicues, each of which was pondered long and thoughtfully.

This ability to entertain himself stood him in good stead on a certain day in November on the way home from our annual visit to my parents in Iowa. It was during my first year at Gardiner and, due to the press of work and activities, my trip had been deferred to a date later than usual.

Elmer and I had made the trip to Iowa in bright, balmy weather, and ten days later, on November 13th, I headed the Metropolitan homeward.

I was intoxicated with the warm, gold-dust beauty of autumn. Elmer seemed to feel it also. Though he ordinarily had eyes only for cities and towns, today he rode serenely on my shoulder and murmured companionable comments on the scenes of the prairie.

In spite of the traffic and occasional towns, Elmer and I rolled along in a world all our own, with a spreading dome of white-laced blue sky above and the plains stretching into the skyline in all directions. As much as I loved being with people, I greedily absorbed all this aloneness and felt a great need to drink to my fill all the privacy the road offered.

We stopped several times to enjoy a bit of scenery or some roadside attraction. Somewhere in Wyoming, I left the highway and spent a long time wandering about an Indian trading post.

Inside, Elmer sat on my shoulder while we admired the bright blankets and the turquoise jewelry. Outside, we looked at a sunbaked old covered wagon with a few shreds of its canvas cover still dangling, and at other faded relics of the pioneers.

I excused myself for our leisurely pace with a mental reminder that I practically never did anything purely for myself. This short vacation would be the last I'd have for another whole year. Today I wanted to prolong the time, stretch out the hours.

However, my father's worried parting words kept coming back to me.

"Remember, Gertrude, it's late in the season and a blizzard can hit mighty sudden out there in Wyoming. You'd better not waste any time!"

I *had* wasted time and now I felt guilty.

As always, when I envisaged the possibilities, I thought of Elmer. What if something dire should happen to me in an accident, and Elmer were thrown out into a big, cold, bewildering world? I could visualize him, his bright little brain befuddled with fear, racing headlong into the wilds of the western prairie.

I reached up and stroked him as we walked away from the trading post. "Guess we better get going, Elmer. I don't want you wrecked in a blizzard."

However, when I scanned the sky, there was only blue serenity, and my uneasiness was allayed. Still, it was time to go, so I put the monkey into his car cage and we sped westward. I planned to drive hard and late to get into Utah before stopping for the night, and we had a lot of Wyoming road to cover. No more fooling around.

We were somewhere outside of Rock Springs when I noticed that the sun no longer hurt my eyes. What a relief!

And then I realized that we were driving into some sort of strange, rapidly developing haze.

Before I could believe it, we were in a whole different world. There was wind. And there was snow. The snow came at us from all directions. We were enshrouded in darkness. My Metro pushed bravely into the storm, though at a drastically wind-slowed pace. The highway was obliterated in no time at all, except where the headlights picked out a patch of road scraped bare by a blast of wind.

I was scarcely aware of the traffic ahead and back of me as I tried to buck that raging blizzard and somehow stay on an invisible road.

Elmer, who had slept for miles, came wide awake as soon as the wind and snow hit us. He clung to the side of his cage and took it all in. This was something new for him. And scary too! At first he chattered with excitement and apprehension. I soothed him as best I could and then gave my attention solely to the road. Elmer finally became silent also. No use trying to communicate with someone who stared straight ahead and said nothing. As it kept getting colder, he finally shut out the whole scene by crawling under his covers.

I have no idea how long I navigated that cloud of driving snow. It was hours. It was forever. I lost all sense of time. I couldn't stop, I had to go on.

At long last, lights glimmered ahead—great, tall lights that spelled out "Little America." Even on an ordinary day, this was considered an oasis in the desert. Now it beckoned to me like the lights of Heaven.

Soon we were inside a room lovely with warmth and brightness. I was surprised to find that it was still early in the evening. Under the stress of driving through the blizzard, I had not been aware of hunger. But now I realized that we needed something to eat. I brought Elmer's cage in from the car, installed him in it, and went to the dining room for a quick dinner and some vegetables for the monkey.

After dinner Elmer sat on my shoulder and hugged and patted me, while I did a little reading and slowly relaxed.

By morning the snow had stopped. The whole landscape was a gleaming sheet of icy white, with curving mounds where cars were buried. The road was starkly devoid of traffic.

I went to the dining room and had breakfast, then brought food for Elmer. Afterward, I took the small broom which

I'd brought from the car the night before and went out to beat, push and sweep until the Metro was uncovered.

About mid-morning, out on the highway, an occasional big truck rolled slowly past, while on the grounds of Little America lanes were being cleared.

I loaded Elmer, our luggage, and myself into the car and took a lane to the garage, expecting to have the chains I carried put on my tires. At breakfast people had told me they would not leave that morning. But there was already a long lineup of vehicles at the garage, most of them also awaiting chains. I waited for a long time, and still there was a line ahead of me.

By now traffic on the highway had increased, and I found out it was only a few miles to another garage down the road. I therefore decided to take my chances without chains as far as that garage.

As it turned out, the chains I carried were the wrong size. Worse yet, I was told that none had yet been manufactured for small cars.

There was no choice but to keep going. If another storm should strike, goodness knows when I would get home. I could neither afford the time off from my work, nor the expense of a long stay at Little America.

Highway 30 was a ribbon of ice. I took it very slowly, trying to remember all the things I was supposed to know about driving on ice.

Because of the cold, Elmer was clad in his warmest clothes and riding beside me on a very thick woolen comforter. His cage had been relegated to the back since the comforter was too big to cram into it.

Elmer stood atop his blanket and viewed all the glittery scenery while I carefully negotiated the icy road. We put several miles behind us without a single skid, so I began to feel more confident and to increase speed. This wasn't bad at all!

We had just reached the foot of a steep incline when a huge truck came hurtling over the top of the long ice-glazed hill that seemed to stand on end directly in front of us.

My newly acquired confidence evaporated in an instant when the Metro suddenly began to slide, then to whirl madly round and round in the middle of the road.

And that monstrous vehicle kept right on coming at us.

By some miracle, I got the car righted and into its own lane seconds before the truck barrelled past.

My sharp-eyed little monk had not missed a thing. He instantly sized up the dangerous situation: our skidding car, the hill, the oncoming truck. In a flash he dove for cover somewhere down in the folds of that thick comforter. There he stayed the whole day long.

I think he operated on the theory that what you can't see won't hurt you. And he wasn't taking any more chances! No amount of talking or coaxing would bring him out of hiding as long as the car was in motion. But when we stopped for food or gas, he came up to daylight, chipper and alert.

As the day wore on, the road changed. Pounding truck wheels had beaten the tracks into rows of slush, while the area between remained glassy slick. This gave me a special problem. The chainless wheels of my small car were not wide enough apart to travel in both tracks. Therefore the wheels on my right were always in slush while those on my left were on slick ice.

An even worse problem was caused by the big tankers and trucks that roared by on their well-shod tires and sloshed me with freezing mud and ice. In spite of the constant, labored swish of the windshield wipers, I could scarcely see. I peered intently ahead and had little time to wonder how Elmer was getting along in his hiding place.

As mentioned, Elmer could entertain himself endlessly with practically nothing. Now he had a whole day just to feel the texture of that woolen comforter and ponder the essence of darkness.

It turned out he did a little more than that.

Once a big oil tanker came thundering down the road, and as it passed, in addition to showering the car with gook, it sent a rush of air up through my heater vent that smelled amazingly sweet and fragrant.

I was dumbfounded. Since when, I asked myself, had reeking old oil tankers smelled of perfume? Then a sudden thought struck me. Could Elmer somehow be connected with this strange phenomenon?

When the windshield cleared a little, I slowed my speed still more and with my right hand reached for Elmer in his dark retreat. He was cuddly warm to my touch and had some object clutched tight in his hands. I pulled at the object and he hung on valiantly. After a protracted struggle, through which he never made a sound, I won. The thing I brought to light proved to be my opened powder compact.

Aha! Here was the answer to the perfumed tanker.

Now I wondered what else Elmer had swiped from my handbag, which lay on the seat between us. I felt again and came upon my billfold, which he had stashed away in a corner of his refuge. Surprisingly, it seemed fairly well in order, except for a few crumpled bills. Knowing Elmer, I surmised he had found something else that was of even more interest.

I put my hand in once more and discovered that he was tightly clutching another object. He had surprising strength in those tiny hands, and held on with great tenacity, again in utter silence. When rescued, it proved to be what I had feared—an open tube of lipstick.

Shortly thereafter, when I pulled in to a gas station, Elmer hopped out smartly, and the howling attendants were treated to a most unusual sight—a tiny creature that clowned at the car window and grinned broadly with very red lips.

The red was rather unevenly applied, I thought.

There were splotches of red on his cheeks and above one eye. When I opened the window a crack, the hands he stuck out in greeting were also bright red.

In addition to all of this, much of his black hair had a peculiar shade of beige—the powder, of course. And on that cold winter day this monk smelled like flowers in springtime.

It took considerable rubbing with Kleenex to remove the heaviest of his makeup. The rest would have to await soap and water that evening.

All that day we drove through a land of pristine white, marred only by the mud-slush tracks of the highway.

Back at the filling station I had put my purse behind the seats, and placed two or three toys between the folds of Elmer's comforter. Whether he played with them or not, I

do not know. I only know that when evening came, and I drove wearily into a motel somewhere in Utah, the monkey popped out of his blanket looking perky and happy. *He* had had a fine day.

≫18≪

Decisions

There were times when I felt disloyal to Elmer, especially on those occasions when I referred to him as "that little pest," "that rascal," "the bane of my life." Such descriptions were true, of course, but not all the truth, for to me he was lovable and delightful, even when performing his most dastardly deeds. But just in case there might be any of those people around who thought it unseemly to show affection for a pet, I played down my regard for the little monk.

One afternoon I had worked for hours at my desk, while the monkey sat companionably on the floor beside me. He too worked—on things from the wastebasket. One of our rules was that Elmer could empty my wastebasket and play with its contents to his heart's content any time I worked at the desk.

Now he minutely examined every single item. Each envelope was inspected to see what it held, the address and the picture on the stamp studied, and then the stamp carefully peeled off and its glue side licked and savored. He found a sheet of carbon paper that was most interesting, nice and smudgy. There was even a small brown bottle with a tight lid and something inside that rattled. (For Elmer's enjoyment I had shoved a button into the bottle on purpose.)

I glanced down from time to time to see how he was doing. Each time he shot a sideways glance back at me with an I-can't-be-disturbed air of importance and went on with his work.

The bottle took some time. First he had to shake it and study it from all angles, and that tight lid had to be unscrewed. But the most fun of all was poking a finger in to feel the enclosed object, then shaking the bottle and gouging inside until he finally got the shiny button out.

When this had been accomplished, there were all those varying sizes of letters just waiting to be "read," and then covered with his own writing. Once a hand tugged at my skirt, and after I had completed the sentence I was writing, I looked down to find Elmer standing upright, holding a piece of paper in one hand and reaching up with the other while he spoke to me in Elmer lingo. I understood the request and promptly handed him a pencil. Then we both continued our work.

After Elmer had written long and arduously, he suddenly decided it was time for a break. He dragged the last item, a newspaper, from the now overturned basket, and he did the thing he had so loved to do since his tiny baby days. He seized the newspaper by one corner and dashed madly back and forth through our living quarters. And each time that spread-out paper swished by, a bright, devilish eye underneath it laughed at me and dared me.

"Well, you've been such a good little fellow all afternoon," I told him, "you deserve a romp." And I took out after him. Occasionally I got near enough to step on or grab a corner of the paper, but Elmer, in high glee, just sailed on, leaving fluttering streamers in his wake. In the turbulence the contents of the wastebasket also got spread out across the room.

During a slight pause I glanced about. No real damage was done, yet the place looked almost as wild as it had the day Elmer escaped from his cage and worked ruination while I was gone.

I'd surely hate to have callers right now, I thought, but considered this unlikely since it was almost dinner time. So Elmer and I continued in our heedless, headlong interlude of fun.

The ringing doorbell stopped us. And the person who stood at my door was the "fashion model" of the community. Crisp, correct, not a hair nor a thread out of place. I faced her with a laughing monkey and a house struck by a paper storm back of me, while I remembered that this woman's house was like herself, perfect in every detail.

The only thing I could do was say, "Come in."

She stepped elegantly through the disorder to the davenport, from which I hastily brushed tatters of paper. I put Elmer in his cage and turned to my guest. With arms spread wide and in pseudo exasperation, I said, "That little hoodlum. This is his idea of having great fun."

I dared not tell her I had also had fun. Yet when I glanced at Elmer, I saw that he sat in his cage and simply glowed. For once he was paying no attention at all to a guest, but his eyes were agleam as he gazed out the window and inwardly delighted in the fun we had shared.

I suddenly felt like a Judas. What right had I to speak disparagingly, even in jest, about this really good little monkey who so appreciated every wee bit of happiness?

My embarrassment over the littered room abated somewhat when the guest chuckled and seemed even to enjoy the results of Elmer's paper race. Yet I was certain it was not a thing she would ever have tolerated in her own home.

Household neatness and order were important to me also, and sometimes seemed essential to my very well-being. Yet here I was, so captivated by a tiny monkey that my housekeeping standards could be toppled by the gleam of a roguish eye.

And it did take precious time to put things aright after such a riotous play session. In fact, taking care of the needs of a monkey, along with those of a fast-growing parish, kept me working almost steadily throughout the whole day, and often far into the night. I felt the strain increasingly, though I didn't anticipate that it was about to become a much bigger problem.

It occurred on a busy Sunday. I had been in meetings at the church from early in the morning until three o'clock in the afternoon. I had started to climb the stairs to the apartment and Elmer, and then I simply collapsed.

From there on I'm not very clear about events. I only know that some time later—a day, two days—the doctor was looking down at me and speaking firmly.

"What you should do is take a whole year off, get a complete rest!"

I don't know what I said in reply, only that I was resistant, feeling that I simply had to get back to my tasks.

At length the doctor relented. "All right then, but you will absolutely have to cut down on your work load. That is, if you want to live!"

For the next month someone else took the Sunday Morning Services, and the other church work waited while I spent most of the time in bed and thought over my situation.

I knew the doctor was right, and I'd have to cut down my schedule. But where? I felt that my first duty was to the people of the parish I had been called to serve, those people who had displayed such loyalty and enthusiasm in our joint efforts to rehabilitate the church. Surely this was no time for their minister to falter.

Then, I began to think the unthinkable.

Would I have to find another home for Elmer? I had to admit that taking care of the little monkey took every bit as much time and effort as having a small child in the house. The only difference was that I did leave Elmer without a baby-sitter. Yet I was forever hurrying home to feed him and see that he had exercise and companionship. It was true that my work load would be lessened without him. But so also, I thought miserably, would my joy of life be lessened.

However, looking at the subject in the light of what would be best for Elmer, I reasoned that if the right home could be found for him—a big "if"—then he wouldn't need to be left alone so much and he could have more exercise.

Elmer's need for companionship and exercise had long troubled me. Sometimes I had to leave him alone for hours at a time, and occasionally for an entire day. I always left lots of food and toys in his cage, so I knew he wasn't hungry and that he played and watched the goings-on outside his window. Yet I also knew that he spent much of his time, lonesome and tense, just watching the door and waiting for me.

I let Elmer out of his cage for a good play and exercise period first thing in the morning and whenever I worked at home, he almost always played on the floor. Nevertheless, I felt that this was by no means enough, since he was a little creature meant to swing from trees and have the run of all creation. In the right kind of home Elmer could perhaps have lots of things he now lacked.

Except! Except that he looked upon me as his very own mother. Would he ever be able to transfer that affection to another? I remembered how he had nearly died of grief during my hospital stay.

In anguish, I broached the subject of giving up Elmer to Palmer. He was shocked but saw my point. Changes had to be made somewhere.

Finally he said consolingly, "Well, let's think about it. In the meantime we can look into the possibilities of a new home for the little guy." Then he added, "But I don't think you'll ever give him up!"

Finding the right home for Elmer was by no means easy, for my standards were strict. It had to be a home where the people truly cared about animals. They must not be the kind who would take the monkey just for the fun of it and then cast him off as soon as they found there was work involved in his care. Also, it had to be a home whose occupants were not all kept away by their work. I even dared to hope that these people, whoever they were, would already have a small monkey. Thus they would be versed in the care and feeding of a monkey, and Elmer would have a companion to play with.

Most important of all, that home had to have a woman to whom Elmer could turn for security and even for authority. So far I had been that one. While he was much attached to Palmer, he went to me first if he needed safety, and he never felt under any obligation to obey Palmer. In fact, he resented loudly any effort on the part of my husband to tell him what to do. Elmer obeyed me most of the time. That is, when I was in the room and watching him—and even when I was absent, if the temptation was not too enticing.

So what could we do about a new home for Elmer? It certainly would not be the zoo. I once took him there just to see what his reaction would be to other monkeys. We stood for some time before an enclosure where there were several similar to him. I held Elmer up so he could see well, but he viewed the whole scene with nonchalance, and showed not the slightest desire to join them. There were too many monkeys in too small a space and he was not impressed. Neither was I. This was not his world. My little monkey now belonged to the realm of people.

Many folk expressed a desire for a pet monkey. But most of them, I feared, would be like the woman in Texas who had stopped me one afternoon and insisted that I sell her my baby monkey. She assured me that she could, and would, pay any price I asked.

"Why are you so eager for him?" I inquired.

"Oh, this little monkey is so cute, and he's *clean*," she replied. "I've seen lots of other monkeys, but they were all so na-a-asty!" She fairly wailed that long, drawn-out "na-a-asty."

I held Elmer close to me as I said, "No, this little monkey is not for sale at any price."

He was not for sale now, either. That would be like selling a member of one's family. I only wanted a home for him where he would continue to love and be loved and have his needs met as fully as possible. But I often thought about that woman. Did she think a clean little monkey just grew that way? Couldn't she understand that even a human being, caged and out of his own environment, would be dirty unless given care?

Actually, Elmer did the best he could to keep clean, even in the confines of his small parrot cage. For example, when his toilet corner was soiled, he would very carefully fold back paper to cover the spot. He didn't want to be "nasty."

Soon after that month of rest, when I had resumed my full load of pastoral work, or tried to, Palmer and I went to a ministerial seminar in a town some distance away. It was warm enough that we could leave the monkey in the car during the meeting. Afterward we took him with us while we went to do a little shopping before starting homeward.

And then it happened! A man and woman, both of them kind and gentle looking, approached us with a mixture of timidity and eagerness. They were Ralph and Anne Jurgena, they told us, and they wanted to know if by any chance we would consider selling them our little monkey.

They explained that for several years they had had two monkeys very similar to Elmer. One, Sammie, had given his loyalty to Mr. Jurgena, while the other, Mitzi, had given hers to Mrs. Jurgena. Sadly, Mitzi had recently died and they were simply lost without her.

"Could I hold your little monkey?" Anne wanted to know. Elmer went to her without protest and looked up at her with round-eyed wonderment while she stroked and talked to him.

I stood there and anguished. Here were two people who obviously loved monkeys and knew what was involved in their care. Ralph was telling Palmer that they lived on a small farm outside of town and were seldom away for any length of time.

"If you let us have him," Ralph promised, "Elmer will spend very little time alone. None, really, since Sammie will always be there for companionship. It might take a little time before Elmer and Sammie become friends, but then again, it might happen right away." They even invited us to their home so we could see where Elmer would live.

Anne urged, "If you will let us take him, you can come see Elmer as often as you like. And if we can't make him happy, you can have him back. We'll even draw up a contract, put it in writing!"

What more could one ask? Everything I had dreamed of for Elmer was being offered. Except the transfer of his affections. And Anne was ready to go all out to win him over. Palmer also was impressed, but he looked as miserable as I felt when he said to me, "Well, Hon, he's your monkey. It's up to you."

I stood in a torment of silence. Elmer was back with me now, his arms locked about my neck, his cheek tight and trusting against mine. The pressure of that small body said, "This is where I'm safe. This is where I belong."

Ralph pushed their case. "We're not rich, but we'll pay you a good price for this little fellow."

I finally choked out a reply. "No, one doesn't sell love. If we let you have him, it will be as a gift—or rather, a loan—till we see how he gets along." I stroked Elmer for a moment before I continued. "I'm certain we can never find better people than you to love and care for our little monkey. But I need some time. I'll let you know my decision soon."

The trip home was long and filled with gloom. It had been one thing to speak of giving Elmer up if the right people came along. It was another to face the reality, now that those right people had appeared. Even Elmer, soaking up emotions as usual, was subdued. He didn't play or watch the scenery, but sat quiet in my lap and frequently looked up at me to ask earnest little questions.

That night there was scarcely any sleep for me, and I dragged zombi-like through the tasks of the following day. I couldn't let Elmer go! I had to let him go! The inner struggle went on and on.

That evening a shy young couple, Frank and Susan, came to talk about their wedding and go over their marriage vows. We had met only recently, and I wanted to get to know them better before the ceremony. However, they were so tongue-tied and ill at ease that I wondered how to proceed. Then Elmer came prancing in. He went to each in turn, clung to their fingers, examined buttons and ornaments, and all the while whistled and chattered his conviction that these were utterly marvelous people.

While sitting on Susan's lap, he suddenly flipped up her skirt to see what was underneath. Sure enough, her petticoat was edged with lace, a lovely ribbon of fine mesh over which he immediately became entranced as he proceeded methodically to work his fingers through the holes. Though the young woman blushed a little, she looked delighted and made no move to disengage him.

Presently I took Elmer from her, put him back on the floor, and gave him a bottle of milk. He tippled down the milk with the usual sly eye out to see the reactions. Then he clowned some more before I put him in his cage. By now both Susan and Frank were laughing and perfectly at ease, so we discussed their wedding and their plans for the future. We talked freely, with no barriers between us. The thought flashed through my mind that it would be hard to tell who was of most benefit to the people of this parish, I with all my working and struggling, or this little monkey with his gaiety and rambunctious celebration of life.

We went over the marriage ritual last. When Susan and Frank had gone, certain words of the vows clung to my consciousness and would not go away. "To have and to hold, from this day forward, for better, for worse, for richer for poorer, in sickness and in health, to love and to cherish, till death do us part."

I prepared for bed but knew I could not sleep. Instead, I put on a warm robe, then took Elmer from his cage. The little monkey's eyes drooped with sleepiness as he draped himself limply over my shoulder, tucked his thumb in his mouth, and made a few contented croons, then fell sound asleep.

While holding him, I silently preached myself a sermon. There are many kinds of love. Yet surely all love, no matter for whom, is just as binding in its own way as that proclaimed in the marriage ceremony. Real love holds for better or for worse, even love for this absurd, wonderful little monkey. You can't give up on loving and caring when the going gets tough. Besides, whose fault was it that the going had gotten tough? Was I trying to play God? If I were too busy to take care of this little creature who loved and trusted me completely, then I was just too busy. It was high time I made some changes, but not with Elmer.

I vowed to cut down on my schedule; also to make life better for the monkey. First on the agenda must be a new cage, large and airy. Elmer would stay with me, and he would stay with all the comforts that could be provided.

⇒19⇐

New Dimensions

The search for a new cage for Elmer led me to a store in a town some distance from Gardiner. Here I came upon another small Capuchin who resembled Elmer in looks only.

With tiny arms clasping a ragged doll, this monkey lay unmoving in the far corner of his cage. I talked to him for a long while, but there was scarcely a gleam of response. The small creature fairly exuded dejection and foresakedness. He seemed to have concluded that the only thing left in the whole world for him was the doll to which he clung.

I asked the proprietor about this monkey and was told "Oh, I guess he has rheumatism. We don't let him out of the cage very often so he doesn't get much exercise."

Thinking about Elmer's daily high-spirited take-over of our house, I could have wept for this little creature who seemingly had never known such freedom and happiness.

Elmer hated to be left alone. Yet here was a little monkey who spent endless long, dark hours by himself: from closing time to store opening at nine o'clock the next morning, night after night, and much longer than that on weekends. No wonder he was withdrawn, unresponsive, and almost immobile.

This pathetic sight immediately called to my mind another monkey I once saw in the downtown area of a southern city. It was on a blistering hot day. I remember thinking that the sidewalk burned my feet right through my shoes when, rising on the hot still air came music and peals of laughter.

I followed the sounds till I rounded a corner and was suddenly in the midst of the music and merriment and a crowd of people all looking down at something. I edged into the group to find the cause of the laughter. There, in a circle surrounded by feet, a small organ grinder monkey danced to the music. In spite of the heat he wore pants and jacket, though his feet were bare against the burning pavement. As he danced, he deftly caught and pocketed the coins people tossed.

I did not join in the laughter for I saw that as this little monkey danced, he watched his master with tired, anxious eyes. The organ grinder's face was stern and his eyes hard. Others who watched the tiny performer seemed not to notice that when the monkey occasionally missed a coin, the man jerked him sharply on the leash and spat out a harsh-toned reprimand.

The crowd continued its hilarity and while admiring the deftness and ability of the little monkey, appeared utterly oblivious to his misery. They showed no awareness that here was a small creature being cruelly exploited.

These memories and the plight of the creature before me prompted me to quick action. Since my inquiries about a cage had proved fruitless, I said goodbye to the forlorn little monkey and sped home as fast as possible to Elmer. Taking him from his cage, I cuddled him and told him what a great little fellow he was. Then I let him run and play to his heart's content.

While Elmer worked off excess energy, I finished some housekeeping duties. Then we both settled down at the desk. The monkey worked on the contents of my wastebasket, while I concentrated on the problem of how to obtain a larger cage. I had searched far and wide and now knew that you don't just go out and buy a monkey cage, or even a facsimile of one. Consequently I decided to find somebody who could build one.

I had the cage all planned. It had to be aluminum for easy cleaning. The dimensions would be four and a half feet high, four feet wide, and two feet deep. It would rest on a sturdy platform eighteen inches high. The upper half of the back would be covered with strong, fine-wire mesh so that Elmer could always see out the window. The front would be composed of four removable doors made of open grill work large enough for the monkey to see out of and stick his hands through. In addition, there would be a sturdy swing, and a hide-away compartment fastened near the top where Elmer could sleep, or get away for privacy when he needed it.

I got out the telephone directory and resolved to make phone calls until I found someone who would construct that cage. I made one call after another to ask, "Do you know of anyone who might build a large aluminum monkey cage?" A long list of "no" answers were disheartening. Then I remembered Jim Worthington, who would likely know nearly every businessman for miles around.

I phoned him. "Jim, could you help me find someone who would build a good aluminum monkey cage?"

His answer was a little slow coming, but he finally said, "Well, yes, I do know such a person. Jules Robinson is the best metal worker in this whole county—but there's a problem."

"What's the problem?"

"To tell you the truth," Jim replied, "Jules has become quite a drinker these last few years. Now he's so befuddled that his business is nearly ruined. He's just not reliable anymore."

In spite of Jim's dark prognosis, I was elated. Here was a lead to someone who could build a monkey cage, and I felt oddly confident that he would do so.

The next day, as soon as I could get away from a women's meeting, I took off to find Jules Robinson's shop in a neighboring town. I was in luck. Jules appeared to be perfectly sober, though there was a weary remoteness about him. Tall, thin, and languid, he draped himself against a piece of equipment and listened to my plea that he build me a monkey cage. I thought I caught a flicker of real interest in his pale blue eyes as I told him about my small monkey and his need for the cage. He took the card of written specifications I gave him, looked it over silently, then put it in his pocket. "Okay, I'll get at it right away," he said.

Sure enough, a few days later I answered the doorbell to find Jules there. He stood stiffly erect. "Gottcher cagche out here," he announced, with a definite slurring of syllables.

"Oh, that's just fine," I said. "Do bring it in." Pleasure warmed me as I began to anticipate Elmer in his new cage.

But what was that contraption Jules was negotiating up my walk? True, I had wanted a large cage, but this was more like a room. I knew at a glance it would never do. It would not even go through the door. But Jules pushed and turned and slid the thing until he got it up on the porch and in front of the door. There he stopped and looked owlishly, first at the cage, and then at the door.

Finally I said, "Did you make a mistake on the measurements? It looks to me as if this is just about twice as deep from front to back as I specified."

No, he mumbled, he'd made it according to the measurements. For a long while he looked from the door to the cage. Finally he turned stiffly toward me to announce, "Your doorsh too narrow. Ish ther 'nother door to thish plash?"

To humor him, I led the way to the back door. Jules regarded the back door solemnly, got out his tape measure and did some measuring. "Thish door's too narrow."

As we came back around the house, Jules swayed perceptibly. He paused to look up at the largest window in the house, the very one, in fact, where Elmer's cage was to stand. I knew what he was thinking: could we somehow hoist the cage up through that window? I also knew it wouldn't work, but in his present condition Jules had to be the one to make the decision.

Finally he proclaimed solemnly, "Windowsh too schmall."

Actually, even if we could have gotten that huge cage into the upstairs kitchen, it would have crowded out everything else. It was impossible. When this fact finally began to penetrate Jules' befuddled mind, I said, "Jules, do you still have that card with the measurements written on it?"

He felt about in his pockets and finally drew out the card. He stared for a long time at the figures, then slowly focused his gaze back to the cage. And the truth began to dawn. The cage was exactly double the size it was meant to be.

My heart ached for Jules, for the huge cage was beautifully executed, sparkled with paint, and there was not a rough edge anywhere. Finally, he pocketed the card and said, "Gotta do it over again." Then he trundled the outsized cage back to his truck.

A week later, Jules was again at the parsonage door. This time, however, he did not stand exaggeratedly erect, but rested his hand against the door jamb, limp and languid as at our first meeting. The cage, beautifully constructed, was already on the porch beside him.

"I think it's the right size this time," he said. Sure enough, it slid easily through the door and up the stairs.

As we came into the apartment, Jules' eyes lit up the moment he spotted Elmer. The monkey, sitting alertly in his parrot cage, watched the proceedings with round eyed interest and chirruped questions.

I showed Jules where the cage was to sit—in front of that large east window in the kitchen. Here Elmer would have a fine view of the street below with its people passing by, and of the steep, tree-studded mountainside that rose as a background to the town. In addition, he would have lots more room to climb and play. Jules went back downstairs to bring the platform, and in no time at all the cage was bolted to its legs and ready for occupancy.

I took the little monk in my arms and told him, "This is for you, Elmer. This is your new cage."

I put a few papers and some toys inside the cage, then put Elmer down on the floor to see what he would do. I had removed a lower door and placed a footstool beneath the opening. The monkey didn't bother with the footstool, however, but shinnied effortlessly up a platform leg and was inside in a flash.

While Jules and I watched, Elmer explored, making small conversational sounds all the while. He first tried the sturdy screen next to the window and became absorbed at poking his fingers through the holes. Then he tried the large, two-inch metal grillwork which made up the front doors. He could run his whole arm through these, with lots of room to spare. Once he grabbed the swing and did some wild whirling acrobatics. Then he climbed across to the hideaway compartment, went inside, inspected it carefully and seemed to approve.

Elmer's happy little chirrups and whistles were heart-warming. He seemed to understand perfectly that this wonderful, shiny structure was just for him.

Jules stood and watched intently while Elmer took possession of his new home. As he watched, that air of aloof weariness slowly dissipated. "You think Elmer likes his new cage?" he asked.

"I know he does," I replied.

Jules continued to stare as though he couldn't pull himself away. I placed a chair nearby and invited him to sit down. He dropped into the chair and continued to observe the monkey. Over and over, he asked, "You think he likes it? You really think he likes it?"

Elmer had been so engrossed in his new cage that he had even forgotten to show off. In fact, he seemed to have almost forgotten that we had a guest. After everything had been inspected and doubly inspected, and he had taken a last mad, exuberant whirl on his new swing, he suddenly sprang to the front of the cage. Clinging easily to the squares of an upper door, he grinned broadly and reached both arms out toward Jules. Jules stood up and extended a finger almost shyly. Elmer grasped the finger eagerly with both hands, looked the man straight in the eye, and chattered joyously.

With the monkey still clinging blissfully to his finger, Jules smiled at me and said, "Yeah, this guy really does like his new hangout."

Here was a good man, as both the monkey and I recognized. Jules' exquisitely wrought metal cage, as well as his own sensitivity as a human being, added new dimensions to Elmer's life and mine.

≫20≪

Fire and Water

Elmer was a real "whiz-kid" monkey, but his inventiveness and curiosity sometimes got me into more difficulty that it did him. One day, I took him from his cage and put him to playing on the kitchen floor. Then I turned to work at my desk which was just inside the wide arch separating the kitchen from the living room.

That day I had to compose copy and cut stencil for the monthly newsletter and this immediately consumed my attention. Much later some inner prompting reminded me that I had better see what Elmer was up to. I looked over my shoulder and saw the monkey up near the ceiling. He sat on the edge of the top shelf where my best dishes were kept and held a fragile antique teacup in his hands.

It was a fetching picture: that tiny, jet-black monkey beneath the white ceiling, holding my blue-flowered cup and gazing calmly down at me.

The cup might be perfectly safe there, but I knew if Elmer decided to carry the cup down, there was no way he could avoid dropping it. All in one motion I whirled around in my chair and sprang toward the cupboard.

However, I'd forgotten that the desk's heavy file drawer was pulled out full length, and crashed to the floor over its sharp edges.

Lying there too stunned to move or think, I finally became aware of two things at once: my right leg hurt badly, and Elmer was now down on the floor looking at me with solemn, questioning eyes. I reached out and gave him a reassuring pat and told him everything was okay.

But as I pulled myself up to a sitting position, I discovered that there was a deep dent in the lower part of my leg and it was swelling rapidly. It was just as well I didn't know then that the leg would give me trouble for years to come.

When I was able to hobble across the floor, I climbed atop a step stool and looked to see what had happened to the cup. It was intact. Elmer had carefully put it back in place before climbing down to investigate what had happened to me.

There was no need to scold him. After all, he was just a curious little monkey who, in his exploration, had found and admired a pretty treasure.

A few days later, Elmer heard strange bumping, swishing sounds from below our apartment. It was apparent that he was frightened as he fired alarmed questions at me from his dark eyes. I picked him up and took him downstairs, along with a batch of cookies and a pot of coffee, so he could see for himself the source of the commotion.

As we entered the large downstairs room I could immediately feel the tension leave Elmer's small body. Loosening his tight hold around my neck, he stood up on my shoulder, grasped a handful of my hair with one hand, extended the other toward the roomful of busy women and began to trill joyously.

The women paused from their work to return an equally happy greeting.

"Hello there, Elmer!"

"Hi!"

"How are you, Elmer?"

Then one by one they came by to shake hands and play with him while they munched cookies and drank coffee.

Here was nothing scary at all. These were his friends. The sounds he had heard had been only the sounds of cleaning, mending plaster, sweeping, tearing off old wallpaper and putting up new.

This part of the old parsonage had not been used for years, except that I had had evening youth groups meeting there before the men built a new addition to the church. Now, however, we were still short of classroom space, and this ancient living-dining room was rapidly taking on life and brightness to serve the overflow.

Back at work, the women talked to me above the noise of their activity. The one putting up the last of the ceiling paper said, "We're going to have this place ready by Sunday. We'll put a divider right across the middle of the room. There's plenty of space for two big classes to meet in here."

With Elmer still on my shoulder, I paused next to the door where one worker expertly brushed air bubbles from beneath a newly hung strip of wallpaper. I looked over that roomful of cheerful, hard-working women and thought to myself, "How very much the world owes such as these."

My musing was interrupted by a yell from the woman working by the door. "Hey there, Elmer! You leave my paper alone!"

Elmer had his fingernails under the new strip of paper and was just beginning to peel it loose. I grabbed his hand and sprang away; then to the sound of bantering laughter, headed upstairs with my small culprit.

I don't remember when Elmer first learned to turn on the water at the kitchen sink, but by now he not only turned on the water but inserted the basket-stopper to keep it from draining out. I began to hide the stopper for fear he would forget to turn the faucet off.

However, that small master of ingenuity immediately figured out what to do about an absent stopper. He went to his basket of toys for a baseball or looked for an orange. Either of these would serve his purpose.

One time I watched while Elmer plugged the drain with his ball and ran the large sink over half full of water, then turned the faucet off and went for a toy. He returned to carefully navigate himself and a large, eight-inch rattle up the handles of the lower cupboard drawers and back to the sink. There, he pitched his plaything into the water, then watched with rapt attention to see what it would do. In this case the toy was half wooden handle and half a bright colored tin with rattles inside. At first it spun around and around on top of the water, then slowly gurgled itself full and sank.

Back and forth, back and forth, Elmer went to the toy basket. Each time after he had labored up the drawer pulls with another plaything, he watched intently to see what this one did when it hit the water. Some sank, "kerplop." Some went down more slowly. Others floated.

After our visit downstairs that day, I sat down at my desk to work on a sermon. As was often the case, it was now late in the week and I must give this study time everything I had. My back was to the kitchen where Elmer, down on the floor, was already playing quietly with his toys. Some three hours later I pulled myself out of my work with an odd sensation that I had long heard water running.

Water!

I whirled around in my chair to see Elmer sitting on the counter pensively gazing down into a sink full of toys. Water was cascading over doors and drawers and onto the linoleum floor. To my horror I saw that a good two inches of water covered the whole east side of the slanting kitchen floor. And we were directly above the now silent room where the women had put in so many hours of hard work.

With visions of soggy plaster bulging and new paper falling, I went into frenzied action. I turned off the faucet and took Elmer to his cage. Then I rushed to the bedroom, pulled a heavy woolen comforter from my bed and threw it over the water on the floor.

When the comforter was saturated and heavy, I pulled it into a big washtub, then finished the floor with mop and towels. At last, I turned up the electric heater to complete the drying process.

I struggled to get the heavy washtub out of the apartment, down the stairs, and along the hall to the old parsonage kitchen where my washer and dryer stood. I got the comforter into the washer somehow, but it was so weighty and bulky that the washer wouldn't handle it, so I dragged it back into the washtub, slid the tub to the back door, and managed to put the comforter into an empty garbage can. It was a sad end to a perfectly good piece of bedding, but in my distraught state of mind, it was the only thing I could think of.

I had taken a quick run downstairs to look at the newly-done downstairs room while the comforter was on the floor soaking up water.

Now I went back to look again. There wasn't a single bit of dampness on walls or ceiling. Then it occurred to me that water might be lying trapped between floor and ceiling and would yet soak its way through, so all the rest of that late afternoon and evening I made frequent trips downstairs to inspect the new paper. I even checked in the middle of the night but to my great relief no wet spot ever appeared.

Elmer had to listen to my "no-no's" a long time that day. I was so alarmed about what might have happened that I felt I simply must make him understand that he could not leave water running. While I worked to clean up the floor, I said over and over, "No, no, Elmer, you left the water running. No, no. Don't ever do that again."

He didn't ever do it again. I was glad of course, yet I was also sad. That little monkey had had such good times playing in the water.

The morning sun angled through the top of the window and slid across Elmer, who hung upside down from his swing, when Nina Wiggins bustled up the stairs. My young neighbor shoved a reddish curl back from her forehead as she said, "Hey, did you hear that preacher guy on TV at 7:30 this morning?"

"No," I replied. "What did he talk about?"

"Well, he tried to prove that humans and animals are not related in any way."

Her blue eyes snapped as she walked over to Elmer's cage and shook hands with the chattering little monk, while she imitated the speaker in a pious, sonorous voice.

"An animal does not reason or think. There is no such thing as an animal who can use tools! There is no such thing as an animal who can build fires! Only man, made in the image of God, can do these things!"

Nina then spoke musingly to the monkey who still clung to her finger. "Elmer, you sharp little rascal! You reason, you use a pry to open heavy drawers. Why, I've seen you do all sorts of things that involved reason and the use of tools—like when you figured out how to plug the drain."

She whirled around and asked me in a half-playful, half-serious tone, "Don't you think maybe this little guy is made in the image of God?"

"Why not?" I replied. "If we think of all goodness as a part of the image of God, then Elmer loves, laughs, plays, shares, and creates happiness. These are a part of goodness. If, like the man says, being able to reason and use tools and build fires makes us God-like, then Elmer almost passes that test."

Nina laughed and nodded emphatically. "I knew that guy
was off beam!"

She turned back to the monkey and said, "Elmer, why
don't you learn to build fires?" Over her shoulder she spoke
hopefully, "You don't suppose he *could* learn to build a fire,
do you?"

"Let's hope not!" I replied. "At least I'm not going to
give him matches and show him how. And all on his own?
Well, this monkey is smart, but not that smart!"

Elmer's favorite place to play, especially in cold
weather, was on his own small rug in front of the electric
heater in the kitchen. There he gathered around him his doll,
rattles, cans, bottles, and other playthings.

Also, he dragged newspapers, his never failing source of
entertainment, over to the play area. Sometimes he scribbled
on them with his pencil. Sometimes he looked critically at
the pictures. Sometimes he made spitwads and poked them
into small bottles and through the holes of rattles, then
examined the effect. But always he ended by tearing the
papers to shreds and curlicues, each of which he held up and
studied intensely. By the time he was through, he had quite
a pile of shredded paper.

Thus he entertained himself for long periods of time
while I worked at my desk. One day I became aware of odd
sounds from the play area. Elmer was making strange noises
unlike anything he had ever uttered before.

I spun around and was confronted with a bonfire blazing
on the kitchen floor!

Elmer marched around and around it emitting sounds
like little Indian war whoops.

I lunged into action and soon got the blaze smothered out. The fire had been on the rug and fortunately had not burned through to the floor.

"What happened, Elmer?" I asked while I cleaned up charred paper and washed smoked toys.

Elmer only gazed back at me with an unfathomable expression. I said, "No, no," a few times so he would know that a fire on the kitchen floor was not the accepted thing. I didn't really scold him, however, because I assumed the fire came about by some freak accident. Perhaps a piece of paper stuck on the grate in front of the heating element and accidently burst into flame. Anyway, it was not likely to happen again.

But it did happen again, several times. On each occasion it was accompanied by Elmer's excited little war whoops.

Now I said "No, NO!" in real earnest, for I knew that he was deliberately setting those fires.

But how?

One day I pretended to be at work at my desk, but covertly watched that little arsonist instead. Then I discovered how he did it.

After tearing up a satisfactory heap of the Oregonian, Elmer took a slender ribbon of it and ever so carefully stuck it through the fine grating of the heater. There he sat, holding to the end of the paper, his small, polished back straight and rigid with waiting. Sure enough, at length the paper burst into flame, whereupon Elmer pulled it out and dropped it on his heap of papers. And he had another fire going.

This time as I sprang to put out the blaze, I scolded severely. If I had been frightened before about what would happen to the parsonage when the monkey ran water all over the floor, I was now doubly frightened at the possibility of the whole thing, occupants included, going up in smoke.

Unlike the water episode, however, I was never able to break Elmer of trying to build a fire. He was simply a small pyromaniac who couldn't control his impulse to start a blaze.

The last time it happened was on a late Friday afternoon. I was hard at work on the Sunday sermon. Since I was scheduled to be with my husband at his church all day Saturday, that sermon had to be completed today.

I don't know why in the world I didn't smell the fire, but I didn't notice it for a long time, so long that the papers had burned to flutters of black carbon, Elmer's wool rug had smoldered through to the floor, and his doll's legs were burned off.

This time Elmer had watched in utter silence. No more war whoops. He had learned, only too well, that in a case like this, silence was the best policy.

Right then I determined never again to work with my back to Elmer when he played outside his cage. I would have unplugged the heater except that we very much needed it for warmth.

It took longer to clean up after this last fire, but finally everything was back in order, except for a brown spot on the linoleum where the play rug had burned through.

After I'd scrubbed and polished that spot to no avail, I proceeded to turn my desk around. This involved removing all the heavy drawers before I could even begin to inch the ponderous desk into a reverse position.

Finally it was done. I again sat down to work. Now my back was to the living room door, but I faced the kitchen on the other side of the archway. Elmer, though at present confined to his cage, would think twice before trying to light a fire right in front of me.

I had just settled down to my work when I heard footfalls on the stairs. Thank goodness, no one had come earlier, I thought.

It was Nina.

"I knew you were going to be awfully busy today," she said, "so I thought this hot casserole might come in handy for your dinner."

It certainly would come in handy. In the excitement I had forgotten all about dinner, and Elmer, being full of the memories of his fire, hadn't reminded me.

As Nina handed me the hot, savory dish, she tilted her small, snub nose into the air and said, "Do I smell fire?"

"Oh, I think not," I replied. "At least, I'm sure nothing in here is burning."

This was true. Nothing was burning *now*. I was reluctant to have Elmer's latest achievement known. Certainly my parishioners had accepted the monkey wholeheartedly and were always impressed with his smartness. However, I could not blame them if they should look askance at this fire-building business.

Nina kept right on sniffing and peering about while I put things on the table and fixed a bit of the casserole, vegetable and fruit for Elmer's dinner. Elmer, having now decided he was hungry, whistled and chattered his anticipation of food.

But Nina was not to be deterred by all our commotion. "I swear I smell smoke," she insisted.

Finally I said, "Nina, please sit down at the table and help me eat your good casserole."

"No, thanks," she replied, "I ate at four o'clock with my husband before he left for the mill. He works the swing shift now, you know. I'm not really hungry, and I don't want to hang around and take up your time. I'm going home just as soon as I'm sure your house isn't going to burn down around you. Maybe you've got a fire in the chimney."

"How could that be," I asked, "when we heat only with electricity?"

"Well, then, perhaps there's a short in the wiring."

"Nina," I pleaded, "will you please sit down with me? I want to talk to you about something."

She sat down reluctantly, still sniffing and looking warily about.

I said, "Do you remember when you asked me if I thought Elmer could ever learn to build a fire?"

"Sure, I remember."

"Well, he's learned!"

"HONESTLY?"

Her blue eyes shown with a mixture of horror and delight while I told her the whole story, including this last, most serious episode. I ended by explaining that I'd been reluctant to tell her or anyone else that Elmer had learned to build fires because I didn't know how folks would take to the idea of a firebug in their parsonage. Our people were wonderfully kind and patient but there were limits to what one could expect them to endure.

"No one else needs to know," Nina replied in a conspiratorial voice. "We just won't tell 'em!"

Then, turning to the monkey, who dropped his orange and eagerly seized her outstretched hand, she said, "Elmer, if we accept the standards of that TV preacher, you have just passed the barrier that separates man and monkey.

"Welcome to the human race!"

≫21≪

Go To Sleep, Elmer

"Go-o-o-o to sleep, Elmer. Go-o-o-o to sleep."

From his early babyhood, when the monkey slept curled tight around my neck, these were the last words he heard each night. The litany was lengthened considerably when he had to learn to sleep alone. And, if it did not always work during those troubled times, at least it seemed to help. Otherwise, he was always susceptible to the go-to-sleep chant.

I vividly recall an incident during the early part of my marriage.

It was evening. Palmer and I were going over some important papers. Elmer, who usually played quietly on such occasions, now seemed restless and keyed up. He snatched at the papers, got in the way, and in general made a little nuisance of himself.

So I scooped him up, removed his shirt and diaper, and put him to bed. Elmer promptly sat up. He knew this was not bedtime, and besides, he never retired for the night

before I did. I then sat down beside him and began in a
sing-song voice, "Go-o-o-o to sleep, Elmer, go-o-o-o to
sleep. You're sleepy, Elmer, you're so-o-o-o sleepy.
Go-o-o-o to sleep, go-o-o-o to sleep."

While Palmer watched, bemused and chuckling, I
repeated this formula several times. Soon a change came
over the little monk. He visibly relaxed and his eyelids began
to droop. Then, as I continued the ritual, his head nodded
while his eyelids grew heavier and heavier. And soon he
toppled over asleep.

Thereafter, at any time, day or night, when Elmer seemed
to need rest, I simply talked him to sleep.

On an evening in May of 1961 I again lulled Elmer to
sleep while my husband looked on with his usual amused
interest. Afterward, I inquired, "Palmer, do you see anything
different about Elmer?"

He said, "Yes, the little rascal's getting fat. Look at his
stomach!"

I slid my hand ever so lightly over the sleeping monkey
and his tight, round stomach. "I hope that's what it is," I
mused. "But I don't know. Lately, there's been something
odd about this little fellow."

Palmer jerked upright in alarm. "You mean you think
there's something physically wrong with Elmer?"

"Oh, it's probably just my imagination," I reassured him.
"After all, he still clowns and celebrates like always. It's just
that…well, for one thing, he doesn't streak in and out of his
cage as he used to. He…he's slower. It seems to be an effort
for him."

For a few moments we brooded over the peacefully sleeping little monkey. Then we both laughed a little as Palmer slapped his own stomach and declared, "Getting paunchy will slow a fellow down every time!"

"Then I'll have to put him on a diet," I said. Though privately I reflected that Elmer was already eating less than usual.

In a few days' time the monkey's condition had changed to the extent that Palmer and I were forced to admit that something was wrong. True, Elmer still laughed, whistled, and chattered when there were people around to watch him. But I observed that in quiet moments he wore an inward, preoccupied air. While he still climbed the doors of his cage and reached out his hands for me whenever I came near, the climbing was now plainly laborious.

My husband and I asked each other in consternation, "Where can we find a doctor for Elmer?" We were reluctant to take him to an ordinary veterinarian, knowing that, except perhaps for kittens, vets were unaccustomed to doctoring any animal so small and delicate as our three-pound monkey. We inquired about every vet in our coastal area and finally found one who had treated a monkey, but he had done it only once.

Nevertheless, on the day Elmer drew back and cried out in pain when I tried ever so gently to pick him up, we eased him onto a soft blanket and rushed him to the small-animal clinic headed by the vet who had once doctored a monkey.

There the doctor "tapped" Elmer's tiny, bloated stomach to remove fluid, prescribed some medicine, spoke a few words of reassurance, and sent us away. However, Elmer did not respond to the medication but grew worse. Two days later we were back at the clinic.

It was Thursday, June 8th, 1961. The veterinarian again drained Elmer's abdominal cavity with a needle-type drain. Then he told his assistant to bring him two shots. One was an antibiotic to fight the infection, the other a diuretic. Elmer, still sharp and observant even in the midst of all his suffering, saw the white coated man coming from the far end of the room with the needles. And he cried out in piercing, horrified screams.

He would have fought and bitten, he would never have submitted to those needles, except for the fact that it was the hands of one he loved that held him—mine.

Oh God, they were mine!

Elmer's luminous, terror-filled eyes beseeched me, implored me, and I wanted to scream myself as those large shots were administered to that tiny body.

We left the clinic shortly after twelve o'clock. Elmer lay quietly in my lap. When Palmer stopped the car in front of a downtown restaurant, I said, "You go in and have your lunch, dear. I don't want to leave Elmer just now."

I couldn't understand why I did not want to leave him. Two days before we had left him in the car while we both went in for lunch.

Palmer opened the car door to leave, but he didn't get out. We both just sat there, not knowing why.

Then, suddenly, our little monkey cried out — two or three small, sharp cries. He rolled great anguished eyes up at me, threw his small arms up and out, stiffened, then grew limp. To all my caressing and calling there was no response.

Palmer quickly started the car and careened through the noon hour traffic back toward the clinic. There was no conversation between us, just one great, aching, yearning hope: hope that our little Elmer had only lost consciousness and the doctor would be able to revive him if we got there soon enough.

The traffic moved at a snail's pace. Palmer passed a ponderous log truck, dodged around a street repair barricade, and raced through yellow lights. Of all this I was only dimly aware, for my eyes were on the monkey as I talked and coaxed and tried desperately to detect some faint sign of life. It simply was not possible that this vivacious little creature would not respond as always to my voice.

When we finally reached the clinic, I rushed headlong into the examining room and held out to the doctor my tiny, limp burden. He immediately administered adrenalin. We all held our breath and waited. And waited. But there was no flicker of movement, no sound but the loud ticking of the clock.

Finally, slowly...blindly...I took Elmer from the table and started toward the door.

The doctor called, "Wait! Don't you want us to dispose of the monkey's body for you?"

Palmer answered firmly for both of us. "No, we'll take care of that ourselves."

Unable to face anybody, we stopped at home just long enough for my husband to phone the pet cemetery in Portland and make burial arrangements for the next day. I stuffed a few things in overnight bags and took from the shelf a new white blanket in which to wrap Elmer. Then, with the monkey cradled in my lap, we traveled the long miles north to Portland. All that night little Elmer's body lay on a chair next to my bed.

The sun sparkled down the next morning. I remember that two solemn little boys stood nearby to witness the burial. I placed Elmer gently on the soft white blanket in his newly made wooden casket. Palmer and I gazed down at him for a long time. His glossy black hair glinted against the white blanket, and his tiny, smooth face looked utterly at peace.

As I bent over him, I murmured, "Go-o-o-o to sleep, little Elmer. Go-o-o-o to sleep."

Then the casket was closed. We placed a wreath of flowers on it. And Palmer performed an interment ritual composed on the spot for a small monkey.

Late that day we returned home and Palmer and I dragged ourselves up the stairs to the apartment—up stairs that had become suddenly bare and steep and dreary. Inside the living quarters stark silence reigned. We listened. The whole house listened for happy chatter, pert remarks, a flurry of swinging. There was nothing.

The monkey cage stood open and vacant except for its small empty bed and a forlorn toy. A heartbreaking reminder of Elmer's love of neatness lay in the far corner of the cage: a segment of newspaper folded firmly over what had been a small wet spot. He had done this last chore in spite of the fact that every movement meant added pain. On the table nearby was a dish, a tiny spoon, and a bottle of medicine.

My arms were strangely empty, like the small swing that hung waiting from the top of the cage.

Always before, this place had seemed to sparkle with light and brightness. Now there was only drab stillness. Previously I had scarcely been aware of the brown circle on the ceiling where last winter's heavy rains had caused the roof to leak. Now that splotch glared down starkly at the basket of playthings and the legless doll lying limp and deserted.

Palmer observed it all with tear-filled eyes, I through a great twisting, constricting pain of hollowness. We reached for each other and clung together in the hushed room.

"Palmer," I asked, "how could such a tiny little thing as Elmer leave so enormous an emptiness?"

It was a foolish question, as we both knew, for such a vibrant personality as Elmer's is not confined to size.

My husband led me to the sofa where we had so often sat and laughed with Elmer. I rested my head on his shoulder and wondered aloud how we could break the news to our church folk and neighbors. Fond as they were of Elmer, I feared they could not understand our grief and someone would say that "after all, he was only a pet."

The reactions of others, however, were secondary to us now, and we both forgot everything else as we huddled together and mourned our loss. A shadowy twilight slowly filled the listening rooms. At last darkness fell. Palmer and I still sat on in the waiting stillness.

Finally Palmer patted me on the shoulder as he said, "Well, Hon, life has to go on." He arose and turned on the lamp as he urged, "Why don't you go over your mail while I fix us a bite to eat."

At the desk I dutifully started in on the large stack of correspondence. When I had a heap of junk mail and emptied envelopes, I automatically sprang up to take them to Elmer. But there was only that empty cage. No Elmer to open envelopes, peel off stamps, lick glue and scrutinize the print. A while later, in the midst of Palmer's supper-making activity, the teakettle whistled. I mechanically rushed toward the kitchen to take it off the burner because the noise always bothered Elmer.

This was a pattern that continued for a long, long time. If I happened to be in a variety store, I found myself looking for a special toy for the monkey. Each time I shopped for groceries, I hunted for sunflower seeds and other foods that Elmer especially liked. At home I seemed to be in a constant state of listening for his voice.

I did not have to tell people that Elmer was gone. They already knew, though I don't know how. As I went about my duties with masked feelings, I got the impression that most people not only knew that I grieved, but they grieved with me. No one ever said, "he was only a pet."

At the beginning, they scarcely mentioned the monkey. Then gradually they began to talk about him.

Little Johnny McGuire stopped me at the front door of the parsonage one day to say, "Gee, I bet it's lonesome up there without Elmer."

I replied, "It certainly is, Johnny."

He said, "All us kids just miss him sumpin' awful!" There was a thoughtful pause and then his face brightened as he continued, "Elmer sure was a good little monkey. He liked to make people laugh, didn't he?" I agreed, and Johnny added, "I 'spect he went to Heaven just like people, don't you?"

"Sure," I replied, "and I wouldn't be surprised but what God has some people even in Heaven who need cheering once in awhile."

Johnny broke in eagerly, "I bet he's up there laughing and doing funny tricks for them right now!"

We chuckled together as we visualized that tumbling, grinning little monkey entertaining the folks in Heaven.

Gradually, nearly everyone who had ever known Elmer either wrote or talked to me about him. As they did so, the sadness invariably blended into laughter.

Chuck Snyder, a mill worker, came up to see me one day. It was the first time he had ever been inside the parsonage. He sat down awkwardly in the chair I offered, glanced at Elmer's empty cage, then began abruptly. "As you know, Reverend, I'm not much of a church goer, but I know this community pretty well. And without that durned little monkey of yours, I wonder if the church would have made it."

He shifted in his chair, thought a moment, and his face lit up with humor as he said, "I remember the first time you and I met. You were standing out there in front of the church below the bell tower and that sassy little monkey was on your shoulder. You both just sort of stood there and grinned at me. I know it sounds crazy, but that's when I decided that maybe preachers were human after all. I mean, how can you be long faced and pious-like with a monkey on your shoulder?

"Anyway, that's when it hit me that it was only right we should all pitch in and make this church a going concern. Lots of others already felt the same way. So it happened.

"I guess you could say Elmer was on that bellrope ringing folks together."

The End

Afterword

Elmer had lived only eight years, a very short life for a Capuchin, who may live to the age of forty. However, in his own forthright, happy way, he raced into countless numbers of hearts to become a uniting influence, and even a shaper of attitudes and events.

Little had I known on that snowy day in Dallas that my tiny, unsought gift would work profound changes within myself; that he would give me a heightened concept of all living things, add tenderness and understanding, and edge my life with joy.

Even now, after all these years, I continue to be enriched in memory by a small black monkey who stands on his head and laughs.

Gertrude Caudill Dealy Sorlien

About The Author

Gertrude Caudill's father moved her family from Kentucky to the rich soils of Iowa when Gertrude was twelve years old. During her first day at the new school, the other kids, especially the boys, laughed at her and told her she "talked funny." At home that evening, Gertrude declared fiercely to her mother, "I will never, never, never marry an Iowa man!"

That particular vow later succumbed to the romances of hardworking, handsome Ray Dealy, but Gertrude's life has been characterized by a fierce determination to accomplish good things.

It's what led her to pursue the ministry in an era when women ministers were nearly unheard of. It's what led her to make a baby Capuchin monkey part of her life. It's also what led her, at age 73, to start the daunting task of writing a book about her life with Elmer, and wait another ten years to see it published.

Another of her outstanding characteristics is Gertrude's sense of humor. What else could account for her ability to laugh at Elmer's antics when they tended toward destruction, and the reaction to people who thought her out of place in the ministry?

"It was when I attended ministerial meetings, and was the lone woman among a group of men that I was most aware of my unique position. The men, not quite knowing what to do about me, laughed and teased and brought jokes about women ministers. I rather enjoyed it and laughed with them, though a clergywoman today would take offense, no doubt, and call such behavior condescending."

In fact, that sense of humor was indispensable when it came to raising a family of three boys in the midst of the Great Depression. Bank failure, drought, and locusts plagued the family on their Iowa farm. But they got through all that. Ironically, allergies to Iowa ragweed finally pushed the family to relocate, as Gertrude's parents had done a generation before. On the first day of March in 1939, they arrived in Washington's rich Skagit (Ska′ jit) County and set up a new dairy farm with their herd of prize Guernseys from Iowa.

It was here that Gertrude added another dimension to her life.

"As far back as I could remember, I had always wanted to be a minister. Even as a child in Kentucky, when the children 'played church,' I took the part of the minister and conducted the singing and preaching...While playing church was a fun game for me, deep down inside it was much more, and continued to be so as I grew older. It seemed to me that God and the unseen world were very near, and all life was sacred, and the way we lived was extremely important.

"As a child, I had felt that my inner urge could never be more than a game since only *men* were ministers. Now I discovered that my denomination had no rule against a woman becoming a minister and even pastoring a church."

It didn't take Gertrude long to fulfill the initial requirements for a license to preach, and soon after, she was called to serve the Blanchard Circuit, a group of five parishes in Northwest Washington. World War II was raging in Europe and there was a real shortage of pastors.

"Initially, I was asked to do the preaching for two weeks while the Superintendent hunted for men to fill that and other positions. I suspect that what he really meant was that I should continue as the permanent minister *if* I could manage it, and *if* the people would put up with me...I knew he had his doubts, and on that, I certainly had mine."

But the people accepted her wholeheartedly.

"They even sent word to the Superintendent to look no further for a minister for them, because they had the person they wanted. They then settled down and took it for granted that it was all right with me. The Superintendent did likewise. Later on he merely chuckled when I told him that each week I felt I had told the people everything I knew."

So Gertrude's dream was fulfilled for a time. The farm prospered, her sons grew up into handsome young men, and though the farm work on top of the church work was hard, it was deeply rewarding.

Then tragedy struck.

On September 28, 1951, life came to a shocking, terrible standstill. Ray died, just two weeks after being diagnosed with acute leukemia.

"It was like losing a major part of myself. I scarcely remember anything that happened after that. And yet I know I went about meeting people, and doing all the multitude of things that had to be done. My young sons did the same."

Again, the determination. If half of her life had died, Gertrude would make the other half a new whole. She would pursue that dream of the ministry to its fullest.

The time was right. Paul, who had married a few months before his father's death, took over the family farm. Ross had graduated from high school and Glen was a Junior.

So off to Dallas they went; Gertrude and Ross to enter Southern Methodist University, and Glen to enroll at Highland Park High School.

"It was probably therapeutic for my three sons and me that we each had to work hard and grapple with new challenges in those days. For me, at least, it left less time for the grief that was always just under the surface, and ready to strike out at any empty interval. I was thankful for the demands of classes and books. While still at home, Ross and Glen had bantered me about going back to school after all those years. Did I think I could 'hack it?'

"One day I heard Paul scold them. 'Now you leave Mother alone. Let her *try!* '

"They were all a little surprised at my 'A' grades."

Life's been a graduate school for Gertrude ever since, with one "A" grade after another, awarded by the grateful congregations of people she served, and by her friends and family. Today she has fourteen grandchildren and five great-grandchildren.

"All this makes me sound pretty ancient, I fear. However, I'm still young enough to enjoy them, and to prepare big dinners for all who are near enough to come."

The dinners, of course, are "A" rated.

Monkey on the Bellrope